I0435002

Strategic Studies Institute
and
U.S. Army War College Press

AUGMENTING OUR INFLUENCE:
ALLIANCE REVITALIZATION AND PARTNER
DEVELOPMENT

John R. Deni
Editor

April 2014

The views expressed in this report are those of the author and do not necessarily reflect the official policy or position of the Department of the Army, the Department of Defense, or the U.S. Government. Authors of Strategic Studies Institute (SSI) and U.S. Army War College (USAWC) Press publications enjoy full academic freedom, provided they do not disclose classified information, jeopardize operations security, or misrepresent official U.S. policy. Such academic freedom empowers them to offer new and sometimes controversial perspectives in the interest of furthering debate on key issues. This report is cleared for public release; distribution is unlimited.

*****

This publication is subject to Title 17, United States Code, Sections 101 and 105. It is in the public domain and may not be copyrighted.

*****

Comments pertaining to this report are invited and should be forwarded to: Director, Strategic Studies Institute and U.S. Army War College Press, U.S. Army War College, 47 Ashburn Drive, Carlisle, PA 17013-5010.

*****

*****

The Strategic Studies Institute and U.S. Army War College Press publishes a monthly email newsletter to update the national security community on the research of our analysts, recent and forthcoming publications, and upcoming conferences sponsored by the Institute. Each newsletter also provides a strategic commentary by one of our research analysts. If you are interested in receiving this newsletter, please subscribe on the SSI website at *www.StrategicStudiesInstitute.army.mil/newsletter*.

CONTENTS

FOREWORD

The United States prefers to fight in coalitions, and has made this clear in both word and deed. Most of the key American national security or defense strategies, such as the *Quadrennial Defense Review* report or the *National Security Strategy*, of the last decade or more note this fact. In practice, the United States worked diligently and tirelessly to construct and maintain coalitions of the willing in both Iraq and Afghanistan. American political and military leaders did this — and will continue to do this for future conflicts — because coalition allies provide both political legitimacy at home and abroad for broad national security policies and specific military operations, and because coalition partners help to shoulder security burdens.

For these reasons, it seemed appropriate and necessary to address the role that allies play today and might continue to play in American national security formulation and implementation during an era of change for the U.S. military, and for the U.S. Army in particular. That was the task given to a panel of experts convened by the U.S. Army War College at the 24th Annual Strategy Conference in April 2013 in Carlisle, PA. Organized and chaired by Dr. John R. Deni of the Strategic Studies Institute, the panel — consisting of Dr. William Tow of the Australian National University, Dr. Carol Atkinson of the University of Southern California, and Dr. Sean Kay of Ohio Wesleyan University — addressed the importance of allied and partner contributions to current and future national security challenges and the most effective and efficient ways for the United States to leverage those contributions in the pursuit of common interests.

The chapters in this edited volume are based upon the presentations of those experts at the Strategy Conference, and the Strategic Studies Institute is pleased to offer them as part of the ongoing discussion over the future of the U.S. Army in American national security.

DOUGLAS C. LOVELACE, JR.
Director
Strategic Studies Institute and
U.S. Army War College Press

CAPSTONE TO ALLIANCES PANEL

John R. Deni

During the many years of America's involvement in Afghanistan, allied contributions from across the globe have been extraordinarily valuable. Admittedly, the use of caveats by some contributing partners created challenges. Occasionally, the military performance of some allies left something to be desired, at least as perceived by some.[1]

Nonetheless, from at least two perspectives, allied contributions were vitally important. First, from a political perspective, allied participation provided political legitimacy for both U.S. domestic and international audiences. Allied participation also allowed the United States to share the political risks with others. Particularly as the conflict there dragged on year after year, having international partners strengthened legitimacy claims and cushioned what might have been a more precipitous drop in public support for ongoing operations.

Second, from an operational perspective, every pair of allied boots in Afghanistan represented a pair that the United States itself did not need to deploy. Counterinsurgency doctrine, which the United States and its allies pursued in Afghanistan particularly since the 2009 surge of forces there, demanded a large troop presence on the ground. In order to reach the troop levels necessary, the United States turned to its allies, and eventually allied troops comprised about one-third of the total foreign troop presence in Afghanistan. The United States may have had the capacity to meet this need itself, but it would have required asking for even greater sacrifice from American Soldiers and their families at a time when Army leaders were routinely characterizing the service as "stretched." During the height of the wars in Iraq and Afghanistan, the U.S. Army had already reached a one-to-one ratio between the duration of each combat tour and the amount of time spent at home station with family and for training. Hence, and given the size of the all-volunteer U.S. military at that time, to generate additional combat brigades for rotation into Iraq and Afghanistan would have required dropping below the one-to-one ratio by shortening time at home station or lengthening combat tours. Moreover, an increase in the number of American troops in Afghanistan at any given time would have substantially increased the costs of operations there.

There is a sense, though, that the war in Afghanistan, as well as the one in Iraq, have together served to almost exhaust the United States as well as its allies.[2] Evidence for this — at least in terms of political exhaustion — has been seen most recently in the 2013 debate over whether to use military force against Syria in the wake of the Assad government's use of chemical weapons against civilians. Despite strong arguments made by the Barack Obama administration officials in favor of upholding the global norm against using chemical weapons, and hence justifying an attack on Assad's forces and infrastructure, there was and is a strong bias against military engagement in distant lands, especially when vital national security interests are not immediately at risk.

Added to this apparent shift in willingness to engage in coalition military operations is the potential decline — or at least the perceived decline — in Western military capabilities. A decade of expensive, distant military operations, plus more recent defense budget austerity in the United States and among most U.S. allies, have combined to sap acquisition efforts over the last several years, as well as compel major force structure cuts. The result is that some question not simply **whether** U.S. allies will a play a significant role in any America-led coalition in the near future—which is largely a political question—but, if so, **how** they will do so, given structural reductions.[3]

Nevertheless, the United States has made it abundantly clear over the last decade or more, including as recently as the January 2012 *Defense Strategic Guidance*, that it prefers to wield military force in a coalition context **and** that it will look first to its allies in Europe as the security partners of choice. For example, the 2010 *Quadrennial Defense Review* (QDR) report noted that, "Whenever possible, the United States will use force in an internationally sanctioned coalition with allies, international and regional organizations, and like-minded nations committed to these common principles."[4] Elsewhere, the report argues that the United States has, ". . . an enduring need to build future coalitions."[5] The more recent 2012 *Defense Strategic Guidance* made a similar point: "U.S. forces will plan to operate whenever possible with allied and coalition forces."[6] With regard to the importance of Europe, that document noted, "Europe is our principal partner in seeking global and economic security, and will remain so for the foreseeable future."[7]

But it is not simply Europe where America finds some of its closest, most capable allies. Australia, South Korea, and Japan each maintain significant military capabilities, although with limited power projection platforms and varying degrees of international ambition. Regardless, Australia has been an important, non-European force provider in both Iraq and

Afghanistan, while Japan and South Korea offered smaller but important medical and reconstruction assistance. Additionally, aside from combat operations all three countries are likely to continue to partner with the United States to build security and stability throughout the Indo-Asia-Pacific region. Japan, in particular, has shown a strong interest in building security ties through peacetime engagement across the region, and Australia has agreed to host U.S. Marines on a rotational basis in Darwin.

Washington is hence confronted with the question of whether, when, and how to collaborate with and leverage the remaining capabilities of critical allies and other partners in the post-International Security Assistance Force (ISAF) environment. This was among the central questions before a panel entitled, "Augmenting Our Influence: Alliance Revitalization and Partner Development," during the U.S. Army War College's Annual Strategy Conference in April 2013. Three expert panelists — Dr. William Tow of Australian National University, Dr. Sean Kay of Ohio Wesleyan University, and Dr. Carol Atkinson of the University of Southern California — were each asked to consider the aforementioned issues, as well as to address how the United States should balance the need to maintain traditional alliances and partnerships in Europe as it places more emphasis on the Indo-Asia-Pacific and what Landpower's role might be in identifying, developing, or maintaining those relationships.

Dr. Tow's presentation, "Pursuing U.S. Strategic Interests in the Asia-Pacific: Pivoting Away From Disorder?" assessed the utility of the rebalancing strategy, the role of allies in that strategy, and the degree to which Landpower might form a critical implementing element. Tow found that most of America's allies and key partners in the Indo-Asia-Pacific region have welcomed Washington's rebalancing, but, at the same time, most are reluctant to embrace it too openly and aggressively. Doing so, argued Tow, could place those countries in an awkward position vis-à-vis China, which has become the most important trading partner for many countries in the region, displacing the United States in the process. In sum, while reaching for Washington's outstretched hand, few countries in the region want to be placed in the position of having to choose between the United States and China. Meanwhile, China views the rebalance skeptically at best, and as a potentially hostile policy of containment at worst. Trying to manage Chinese perceptions, while engaging traditional allies and new partners, will be among Washington's chief challenges in the coming years. The role of Landpower in all of this, argued Tow, may be severely limited thanks to sequestration and defense austerity, relegating most of the military components of the rebalance to the Air Force and the Navy.

One area where Landpower may play a critically important role though, even under conditions of austerity, is in terms of security cooperation, and especially combined education. Dr. Atkinson made just this argument in her presentation, "Military Soft Power in the 21st Century: Military Exchanges and Partner Development," in which she posited that the ability to co-opt, persuade, and influence the thinking of others ultimately supports international peace and stability. U.S.-hosted military educational exchange programs provide a vitally important means of building individual relationships that form the basis for bilateral and multilateral partnerships among the militaries of different countries. Atkinson cited data that indicates the officers who come to study at U.S. military educational institutions are likely to reach positions of power in their home countries, and that most of the officers return home with positive impressions of the United States. Hence American Landpower — and especially Landpower schoolhouses — plays an important role in facilitating not simply the transfer of doctrinal or factual information, but also the development of positive, beneficial relationships that help to shape the security environment.

Whether or not the United States is employing Landpower in a strategically coherent fashion in Europe specifically was the subject of Dr. Kay's presentation, entitled "Rebalancing and the Role of Allies and Partners: Europe, NATO, and the Future of American Landpower." Kay argued that cuts to U.S. Army forces in Europe make sense, but only in the context of a carefully thought out strategy. In his view, failure to align military cuts with strategic goals risks further erosion of the transatlantic security architecture and misses an opportunity to gain more operational capacity from America's allies and partners. If Washington can properly incentivize its European allies — for example, by **further** reducing its presence in Europe and by allowing a European to hold the top military position in the North Atlantic Treaty Organization (NATO) — it may yet succeed in spurring its allies to invest in increased crisis management and expeditionary capabilities. American Landpower, facing a challenging era of defense austerity in the coming years, can play a supporting role in this regard.

These three compelling presentations were based upon the chapters that follow in this edited volume. Together, they provide important insights for considering whether and how the United States will wield

Landpower in coordination with, and in support of, its allies and partners around the world in the advancement of common security interests. The answers to such questions are vital to the U.S. Army specifically, and the United States more broadly, as it contemplates the role of Landpower in a post-Afghanistan era characterized by decreasing defense budgets and contracting end strength.

ENDNOTES - CAPSTONE

1. Jason Motlagh, "For U.S. Troops in Afghanistan, Coalition Forces are Mixed Blessing," *Time*, December 8, 2010.

2. See, for example, Zbigniew Brzezinski, *Strategic Vision: America and the Crisis of Global Power*, New York: Basic Books, 2012.

3. See Stephen J. Flanagan *et al.*, *A Diminishing Transatlantic Partnership? The Impact of the Financial Crisis on European Defense and Foreign Assistance Capabilities*, Washington, DC: Center for Strategic and International Studies, 2011.

4. U.S. Department of Defense, *Quadrennial Defense Review Report*, Washington, DC: U.S. Government Printing Office, February 2010, p. 10.

5. *Ibid.*, p. 74.

6. U.S. Department of Defense, "Sustaining U.S. Global Leadership: Priorities for 21st Century Defense," Washington, DC: Department of Defense, January 2012, p. 4.

7. *Ibid.*, pp. 2-3.

CHAPTER 1

PURSUING U.S. STRATEGIC INTERESTS
IN THE ASIA-PACIFIC:
PIVOTING AWAY FROM DISORDER?

William T. Tow

America's role as an unrivaled global hegemon may well be ending. There is little consensus in the United States or abroad, however, on what type of international order or disorder is replacing it, or how Washington and its allies should respond. Yet the stakes for realizing success in future U.S. and allied grand strategic policy in what is becoming a more complicated and diffuse geopolitical environment could not be greater, and the challenges impeding such success are no less daunting. An "apolar world" following a relative U.S. decline in world power could result in international anarchy, precipitate regional conflicts, intensify ethno-religious strife, and reverse the positive effects of globalization. If these outcomes are not avoided, the Eurasian land mass, which has dominated modern international relations and order-building for centuries, could slip into what Niall Ferguson has characterized as a "New Dark Age."[1]

No development more embodies the challenge to U.S. primacy than the rise of the People's Republic of China (PRC). Optimists such as Zbigniew Brzezinski and former Australian Prime Minister Kevin Rudd anticipate that China and the United States can and will co-exist as "giants, but not hegemons." They argue that both America's capacity for self-renewal as an Atlantic and Pacific power and China's need to couple its economic growth with more sophisticated social and political adjustments in Chinese society will invariably drive the two countries toward effective mutual engagement.[2] Pessimists point to both China's assertive nationalism and its historical patterns of power politics leading to mistrust and balancing behavior among great powers as evidence that any such *modus vivendi* is a remote prospect.[3]

Recent fiscal constraints notwithstanding, evidence is growing that the more pessimistic view about China's interests and intentions relative to America's own is gaining traction. In late-2011, U.S. President Barack Obama announced that the United States would respond to the PRC's growing military power by adopting a posture of "re-balancing" or, as it has become more commonly labeled, a "pivot strategy" in the Asia-Pacific region.[4] This new posture was introduced as a comprehensive American response to intensifying geopolitical change in the Asia-Pacific region by ensuring that the U.S. strategic presence there would be substantial and enduring despite U.S. and the world's ongoing financial crises. To support this objective, the United States would increase the Pacific component of its total international naval deployment power from 50 percent to approximately 60 percent by 2020. It would expand rotational deployments of U.S. Marines to Australia as one part of a more concerted effort to pursue greater regional force projection capabilities. It would pursue free trade in the region via the promotion of a Trans-Pacific Partnership (TPP) initiative. It would become more engaged in Asia's multilateral security and diplomacy politics. The U.S. Department of Defense (DoD) justified Obama's initiative when it released a *Strategic Guidance* statement in January 2012. This document underscored that:

U.S. economic and security interests are inextricably linked to developments in the arc extending from the Western Pacific and East Asia into the Indian Ocean region and South Asia, creating a mix of evolving challenges and opportunities. Accordingly, while the U.S. military will continue to contribute to security globally, we will of necessity rebalance toward the Asia-Pacific region.[5]

Although China was clearly the major catalyst for its adoption, the pivot strategy has actually been represented by its architects as more of a demonstration of U.S. resolve for remaining a key politico-strategic force in the Asia-Pacific rather than targeting any potential rival. They even insist that, if properly implemented, the pivot could facilitate the finding of common ground with China and underwrite cooperative relations with that country where the two countries' interests converge. America's rebalancing initiative is thus intended, as the President's national security advisor observed in late-2012, to be a strategy for embracing Sino-American cooperation whenever possible, while acknowledging that Sino-American differences will inevitably occur over some issues.[6] This remains the case, they insist, despite the pivot strategy's critics insistence (both in Asia and the West) that it merely reflects the latest American efforts to revive the Cold War by targeting China as an inevitable American adversary and to pursue a hegemonic strategy to reinforce Washington's desire for the Pacific to remain "an American lake."[7]

More concrete policy questions about the pivot strategy than those entwined in zero-sum logic have since emerged, along with questions regarding the implications for American Landpower. It is true that most U.S. regional allies and partners have generally welcomed the American re-balancing initiative as a potential counterweight for what they view as intensifying Chinese nationalism and geopolitical assertiveness.[8] Yet, they simultaneously worry that Washington will insist that they be too open in criticizing or confronting the Chinese on sensitive regional security issues. China, unsurprisingly, has been more skeptical — with various analysts in that country often arguing that the U.S. pivot strategy is merely an updated version of the Cold War containment strategy directed against China. Official Chinese government statements have been relatively restrained while "nonauthoritative" commentary from retired military officers, media or think tanks has been more hostile.[9]

Some key policy challenges and patterns are emerging that should provide a basis for determining how useful and relevant U.S. re-balancing strategy will be and whether and how U.S. Landpower might be an effective tool in achieving that strategy. Two such challenges will be discussed here: (1) how to facilitate U.S. overarching policy interests in the Asia-Pacific relating to the pivot strategy; and (2) how to link those interests to America's overall geopolitical interests directed toward Eurasia, with emphasis on how U.S. and allied strategy, military deployments, and Landpower capabilities could be affected in an era of increasing austerity. A viable regional/global U.S. strategy nexus, successfully prioritizing and earmarking U.S. strategic resources within Eurasia, will become increasingly challenging during a time of intensifying and painful fiscal constraints.

THE PIVOT STRATEGY AND
U.S. GEOPOLITICAL INTERESTS

Separated from Asia and Europe by two vast oceans and blessed with more navigable internal waterways and connecting arable land than any other country, the United States has been and remains the world's unrivaled maritime power. Its fundamental security has been underwritten by the projection of sufficient naval (and air) power to control the ocean approaches to North America, to protect its international maritime supply lines and, when required, to dominate critical Eurasian confluences and chokepoints through the waging of successful expeditionary warfare.[10] The U.S. Marines were created to protect U.S. naval elements against raids by hostile parties and to carry out similar operations against selected adversaries during naval operations. The U.S. Army was originally formed to defend the long U.S. eastern coastline, and operate in the country's expanding western frontiers. Both of these services later expanded their missions to include both large-scale conventional fighting in overseas combat areas and counterinsurgency operations.[11] They did so, however, to supplement the predominantly U.S. offshore power projection strategies underwritten by naval capabilities and later by airpower to ensure security of the North American homeland (and, by extension via the Monroe Doctrine, the Western Hemisphere) and to preserve U.S. global commercial interests through ensuring American control of the world's oceans.

Over the past 7 decades, Washington has expanded upon these two missions by adding a third: the prevention of any Eurasian continental power emerging in ways that could challenge U.S. global primacy. Russia and China are often nominated as the most likely such peer competitors. However, Russia's inability to overcome a poor climate that limits its agricultural production and distribution infrastructure, and the permeability of its geographic boundaries, constrain its power. China's interminable social problems have combined with a lack of maritime assets and reach to render it thus far unlikely to match or overtake its American rival over the short term. The United States, by contrast, has been able to deploy its Landpower in ways to contain the Soviet bloc from expanding throughout all of Europe during the Cold War. It has stationed a sufficiently effective combination of land and offshore assets in East Asia to prevent China from projecting its strategic assets beyond its own peripheries and into the broader central/eastern Pacific.[12]

The Barack Obama administration's adoption of the pivot strategy merely confirmed what was already obvious to all: The Asia-Pacific or broader "Indo-Pacific" region is emerging as an increasingly critical element of contemporary international relations and therefore as a key component in American global strategy. "Core" American interests are clearly embedded in the pivot strategy initiative. These include: defending the U.S. homeland from emerging regional threats (i.e., long-range Chinese and burgeoning North Korean nuclear weapons systems); preventing great power wars (such as between China and Japan) that could spill over to undermine U.S. strategic and economic viability; maintaining allied security; preventing or at least containing the spread of weapons of mass destruction (WMD); ensuring an open and liberal international trading system; and advancing democracy or political liberalization throughout the Asia-Pacific region and internationally.[13]

In March 2011, U.S. Assistant Secretary of State for East Asian and Pacific Affairs Kurt M. Campbell reiterated a five-pronged approach the administration has embraced to protect these interests. Geopolitical components of this approach include: (1) deepening and modernizing U.S. bilateral security alliances in the region; (2) broadening U.S. engagement with other "regional strategic partners" such as Indonesia, India, New Zealand, and Singapore; (3) pursuing a "predictable, stable, and comprehensive" Sino-American relationship; (4) ensuring meaningful U.S. participation in the region's emerging multilateral security architecture; and (5) sustaining a "confident and aggressive" U.S. trade and economic strategy. Campbell linked soft power policy components such as promoting democratic values, human rights, and the rule of law in the region to these five "hard power" components.[14] The pivot strategy, as it evolved throughout late-2011 and 2012, was designed to project and sustain U.S. influence in an Asian region that has intermittently questioned the American will to consistently do so over time.

To what extent have these five components underlying the success of the pivot strategy been successfully realized? To date, the record has been mixed. For example, U.S. budget cuts resulting from sequestration and other austerity measures, coupled with other strategic and diplomatic factors, have complicated U.S. strategy. In terms of "Landpower" capabilities, for example, plans to reduce the U.S. Army's active duty strength from 570,000 to 490,000 clearly affect the United States' ability to conduct large-scale operations. Yet, in 2011, the U.S. defense budget remained nearly twice as large as the next nine countries combined ($739.3 billion versus $486.54 billion) and was sustained at parity levels with Cold War defense spending.[15] It is evident, however, that the Obama administration has attempted to combine military capabilities with the broader diplomatic and economic measures required to realize the pivot strategy's basic objectives.

Modernizing Bilateral Security Alliances.

Washington's "modernization" of relations with its bilateral allies has been marked by a series of countervailing trends. Japan—often characterized as the "lynchpin" of U.S. strategy and force presence in Asia—remains home for approximately 38,000 U.S. military personnel (including 2,000 Army, 18,000 Marine, 6,000 Navy, and 12,000 Air Force personnel), 43,000 military dependents, and 5,000 U.S. DoD civilian employees. Shaped and updated by intermittently changing Guidelines for Japan-U.S. Defense Cooperation and Japan's National Defense Program Outline, the U.S. Forces Japan mission is to develop plans for the defense of Japan and "if contingencies arise, to assume operational control of assigned and attached U.S. forces for the execution of those plans."[16] The recent shift in Japan's defense posture toward developing a more "dynamic deterrence" strategy to facilitate that country's ability to respond to a wider array of contingencies, and to work more closely with the United States and other possible defense partners, has been welcomed in Washington.[17] So, too, has the willingness of Japan's Ground Self Defense Force (GSDF) and its Central Readiness Force to upgrade its training with U.S. Army Japan in the aftermath of the March 2011 Tohoku earthquake to enhance force mobility, command and control, and other operational capabilities for both conventional military contingencies and broader security missions such as disaster relief.[18] Intra-alliance tensions, however, are fueled by the long-standing resistance of substantial portions of the Okinawan populace to the U.S. military presence and operations on that island and, more recently, by intensified U.S. concerns over the Japanese Prime Minister Shinzo Abe government's assertive nationalism applied toward its differences with China over territorial issues in the East China Sea.

U.S.-South Korean security ties warmed noticeably during President Lee Myung-bak's administration (2008-12), and there is no evidence this will change under his successor, Park Geun-hye. Since her ascension to office in early 2013, for example, there has been a slight increase in U.S. Landpower deployed in the Republic of Korea (ROK) (up from 28,000 to 30,000 U.S. forces), more intense and diverse military exercises between the two countries' military components (including the first large-scale river crossing training in more than a decade) and the deployment of the U.S. Army's 23rd chemical battalion (also capable of operating in nuclear and biological warfare environments) to a base north of Seoul. More broadly, there is nearly unanimous support for the U.S.-South Korea alliance in the latter country (80-95 percent according to recent polling) as the North Korean nuclear threat intensifies. However, a strong majority of South Koreans—62 percent—regard Japan as a threat to their country.[19] South Korea's wartime memories and ongoing territorial disputes with Japan, undercut American desires for greater intra-allied collaboration in Northeast Asia. South Korean reluctance to assume wartime command of allied forces by 2015, the evolving nature of U.S. extended deterrence guarantees in the region as North Korea develops its nuclear capabilities, and Seoul's concern that it may be distancing itself too much from China as its major trading partner and as a moderating force vis-à-vis North Korea, are other sources of future stress between the United States and its South Korean ally.[20]

President Obama's initial address outlining how the United States would execute the pivot strategy was delivered in Australia. That ally's assent to host rotational deployments of U.S. Marines constitutes a core element in the strategy's implementation. So, too, does the recent participation of Royal Australian Air Force personnel in training exercises with U.S. and Japanese counterparts in Guam, the 3-month embedding of an Australian *Perry*-class frigate in Yokosuka, Japan, to patrol as part of the USS *George Washington* Carrier Strike Group, and Australia's hosting of exercise Southern Jackaroo in May 2013 — the first ground exercise involving the three countries held in that country. As in the case of South Korea, a large majority of Australians (74 percent) supported the President's initiative. Those who did not cited prospects of China punishing Australia by diverting its substantial trade away from it or of Australia getting caught between its American security ally and its increasingly dominant Chinese trading partner in a future Sino-American confrontation.[21] Australian policymakers understand that, apart from the shared values which underscore Australia's relations with the United States, their country could not possibly establish the scope and depth of security ties with the PRC that it has developed over the past century with the United States. They also know that the pivot strategy highlights Australia's importance to the United States as an ally which can project substantial and positive influence throughout Southeast Asia—an area where China has recently made a major effort to gain strategic leverage at U.S. expense. As Peter Jennings, director of one of Australia's most respected think tanks on defense policy recently observed:

> While in the past Australia's geography made it too remote to be useful other than as a location for intelligence collection, Darwin in the north and the port facilities of HMAS Stirling in Western Australia now offer the means for the United States to sustain a more substantial presence in Southeast Asia and the Indian Ocean.[22]

The Philippines and Thailand remain Washington's two formal security allies in Southeast Asia, yet both have oscillated between embracing and distancing themselves from U.S. power. The so-called global war on terror launched in the aftermath of September 11, 2001 (9/11) was a catalyst for the warming of these two bilateral alliances after both the Philippines and Thailand had distanced themselves from the United States during the 1990s. Filipino nationalism—leading to the U.S. departure from its basing operations in that country—and Thai propensities to "bend with the wind" toward aligning more with the perceived rising regional power (China), had worked to render uncertain the context and future of the two countries' mutual defense treaties with the United States. During the years immediately following al-Qaeda's attacks on American soil, however, Filipino and Thai policymakers worked with their U.S. counterparts to combat jihadist forces throughout Southeast Asia—the designated "second front" where the forces of international terrorism had made serious inroads. The containment of the extremist Abu Sayyaf terrorist group on the island of Basilan during 2002-03 and the capture of Hambali, a top al-Qaeda operative, near Bangkok in August 2003 were illustrative. However, such collaboration generated robust criticism within both the Philippines and Thailand. Filipino critics argued, for instance, that the presence of U.S. forces in such joint exercises and operations such as *Balikatan* conducted in Mindanao was unconstitutional and could only aggravate the Muslim population in the southern Philippines.[23] Nevertheless, U.S. officials have negotiated an accelerated schedule of joint training exercises including a more extensive rotational presence of U.S. forces in the country and the U.S.-Philippines Mutual Defense Treaty has been formally reaffirmed.[24] The latest *Balikatan* exercise conducted in April 2013 was particularly noteworthy in emphasizing Landpower projection capabilities. U.S. Army spokesmen underscored the training objective as developing the Armed Forces of the Philippines' rapid deployment capability to deploy forces anywhere in the Philippines archipelago over 4 days (within a projected time frame of 6 years) and to conduct "a full spectrum of combat operations."[25]

Many Thais have regarded the United States more skeptically since the 1997 Asian financial crisis when, from Thailand's perspective, Washington failed to assist a reeling Thai economy. China offered Thailand modest economic assistance, restrained from devaluing the *renminbi* which would have damaged the Thai *baht* even more severely, and surpassed the United States as Thailand's second largest trading partner in 2007. In 2010, Thailand declared a strategic partnership with China. This contrasted to the U.S. application of sanctions against Thailand following the latter country's military coup in 2006; Thai politicians' criticism of perceived U.S. intervention in their country's domestic politics as a self-appointed mediator in clashes between the Thai "red-shirt" and "yellow-shirt" factions following Prime Minister Thaksin Shinawatra's exile; and Thailand's refusal of a U.S. request to use the U-Tapao base for atmospheric studies that was viewed by many Thais as a cover for U.S. military operations.[26] President Obama's November 2012 visit to Thailand was, however, received favorably and a new "joint vision statement" was signed by U.S. Secretary of Defense Leon Panetta 3 days earlier. Nevertheless, the extent to which the latest U.S.-Thailand reaffirmation of their bilateral security ties reflects actual substance over cosmetics remains to be determined.

Broadening Regional Partnerships.

Widening the network of U.S. security ties to include other appropriate security partners as part of the Obama administration's pivot strategy entails a different set of challenges. Unlike its more formal bilateral relationships with well-established and concrete instrumentalities for negotiation and management that exist to adjudicate intra-alliance interests and differences, the U.S. security ties with informal partners are usually less concrete and based on collaboration over specific issue-areas.

Three such partners currently are notable as pivot strategy collaborators. India, New Zealand, and Singapore are able to contribute to the security of U.S. global interests in tangible ways. India was designated by the January 2012 U.S. DoD *Strategic Guidance* statement, for example, as a "regional economic anchor and provider of security in the broader Indian Ocean region."[27] It has developed limited interoperability, through the *Malabar* joint military exercises, with U.S. naval units and through mutual disaster relief efforts. The U.S. Army and its Indian counterpart are scheduled to hold a joint military exercise highlighting amphibious operations in southern India during September-October 2013.[28] It sustains a healthy arms procurement relationship with U.S. defense manufacturers.[29]

The United States explicitly signaled that it considered New Zealand to have become a part of its regional re-balancing strategy when U.S. Secretary of State Hillary Clinton signed the Wellington Declaration when visiting that city in 2010. This development was, from Washington's perspective, a logical geopolitical response to China's increasingly active role in the South Pacific. There was an acknowledgement by both sides that the two countries' disagreement over the role in the region of nuclear armed or capable ships and aircraft could be finessed in the interest of reconstituting better strategic relations.[30] Landpower coordination has recently been upgraded, with the New Zealand Defence Force (NZDF) conducting a joint exercise— *Alam Hafa*—in New Zealand's North Island with U.S. Army and Marine Corp and Australian Army counterparts in May 2013, focusing on peacekeeping and counterinsurgency scenarios. Although *Alam Hafa* has been conducted by the NZDF with Australian contingents since 1998, U.S. participation has been secured only during the past 4-5 years.[31]

In July 2005, the United States signed a Strategic Framework Agreement for a Closer Cooperation Partnership in Defense and Security with Singapore. While the terms of the agreement were not publicly disclosed, it is thought that it strengthened already existing arrangements for U.S. ships and combat aircraft to access that city-state's military facilities and authorized greater levels of defense technology sharing.[32] The Singapore Army and the U.S. Pacific Command (USPACOM) have well-developed relations through professional exchanges and such military exercises as Lightning Strike and Tiger Balm that rotate between Singapore and Hawaii and which focus on urban operations and on training in counter-improvised explosive device operations.[33]

The history of security relations between the United States and these informal partners has not always been smooth, and current differences still provide an element of caution in their management. India remains a self-declared nonaligned power and is still at odds with Washington over various diplomatic and military issues. These include legislation over the liability of nuclear accidents in India precluding American companies from fully participating in India's civilian nuclear development, lagging defense trade in recent years, and problems in reaching consensus on various foundational agreements for strengthening defense ties.[34] To date, the China factor appears to be insufficiently compelling to project Indo-U.S. strategic relations into truly more comprehensive levels of cooperation.

Caution also conditions New Zealand/U.S. relations, notwithstanding Wellington's recent joint declarations with the United States on improved bilateral security ties. It has adopted a much softer line toward the PRC on various issues than those in Washington concerned with China's rising power would find acceptable. It has entered into a tripartite agreement with China and the Cook Islands to render aid for improving the water quality in that small Pacific island nation. It has insisted that China be allowed to enter the TPP agreement as a means of avoiding Beijing's isolation or the forging of a regional containment posture against it. New Zealand has explored strengthening a Regional Comprehensive Economic Partnership (RCEP) initiative with the Association of Southeast Asian Nations Plus Three (ASEAN + 3), Australia, and India—a framework that excludes the United States and other non-Asian members of the TPP.[35] Moreover, it remains solidly committed to its anti-nuclear posture which still impedes a full return to pre-1986 defense relations with the United States before New Zealand's de facto abrogation from the Australia, New Zealand, United States (ANZUS) alliance.

As another highly developed but small state, Singapore remains sensitive to the need for maintaining a balance in its relations between China, its Malay neighbors, and external powers such as the United States. Accordingly, as a small city-state with a 78 percent Chinese population, Singapore is unlikely to ever directly oppose China in a future regional conflict, and this may partially explain why it declined a 2003 offer by Washington to be granted a Major Non-North Atlantic Treaty Organization (NATO) Ally status (an offer that the Philippines and Thailand accepted).[36]

Relevant in all three cases discussed here is the improbability that the U.S. Congress would ever ratify a formal bilateral defense treaty with another country some 7 decades into the post-World War II era, leaving successive presidential administrations to pursue security ties through more informal arrangements such as memoranda of understandings or "coalitions of the willing" forged in response to specific issue-areas.

The Pivot Strategy and Stable Sino-American Relations.

The most important determinant of the pivot strategy's ultimate success is the extent to which China can accept Washington's assurances that a permanent U.S. presence and influence in the Asia-Pacific has broader and positive diplomatic and economic ramifications than merely reinforcing military strategy and alliances. That acceptance, in turn, will be predicated on China's ability to convince its regional neighbors that their uncertainties about a China-dominated region are unwarranted, and that a China growing strong will play to their own national interests over the long term.[37] A positive outcome to this process means that China and the United States could conceivably work together toward defusing regional security dilemmas and flashpoints. Skeptics insist that:

> [I]t would not be easy for Obama to explain to the Chinese people that America's military repositioning in the Asia-Pacific is not meant to contain China — because countering China is exactly the aim of America's pivot toward Asia. Any serious suggestions to the contrary are either strategically blind or downright disingenuous.[38]

Several test cases for how effectively China and the United States can work together to stabilize regional stability are emerging. North Korean nuclear developments constitute the most urgent crisis. War avoidance will require delicate coordination between Beijing and Washington to avert another conflict on the Korean peninsula and, if war does break out, containing such a contingency from spilling over to affect Japan and the rest of Northeast Asia. Both China and the United States have strong interests in avoiding a renewed Korean conflict. China's domestic imperative for pursuing sustained economic development and domestic political reform uninterrupted by external conflicts is becoming increasingly apparent. This is true notwithstanding powerful factions within the People's Liberation Army (PLA) clamoring to support North Korea as a means of advancing Chinese nationalism. Exhausted from its involvement in two protracted conflicts in Afghanistan and Iraq and from its role of leading the global war on terror, a financially drained America is hardly prepared to wage another large-scale military operation in Korea.

At first glance, North Korea's Landpower is formidable, given its million-plus person army, numbers of tanks, aircraft, and ships, and its vast array of artillery capable of decimating Seoul. It fields the world's fourth largest army (behind China, the United States, and India) comprising approximately 5 percent of the country's population (1.2 million out of 24 million). Yet, its true capabilities for sustaining any invasion it may initiate against South Korea below the threshold of introducing WMD remain dubious. Most of its conventional weapons systems are clearly outdated. It has lacked the fuel, training, and money to underwrite viable defense modernization programs, opting to divert scarce resources into its nuclear programs—it concentrates on building such asymmetric capabilities as information warfare, ballistic missiles, long-range artillery, special-operations forces, and WMD.[39] It adheres, unfortunately however, to a military posture featuring a high level of politico-military risk. The alleged North Korean torpedoing of the South Korean corvette *Cheonan* and the shelling of the South Korean island of Yeonpyeong in March and November 2010, respectively, are illustrative.

An assessment offered by the International Institute for Strategic Studies (IISS) almost a decade ago still seems relevant in describing the current force balance on the peninsula. U.S. military contingents stationed in South Korea—now numbering around 28,500 military personnel—along with approximately 650,000 active-duty South Korean troops could withstand a North Korean conventional military invasion. But pre-emptive strikes against North Korea of the type that now seem to increasingly be shaping South Korea's defense posture would be fraught with steep risks including the prospect of escalation to a wider conflict. These risks include possible Chinese military intervention on North Korea's behalf (a formal security treaty originating in 1961 is still technically in force), and North Korea's introduction of WMD to inflict maximum damage against Seoul, South Korea's other urban areas and more distant targets in Japan and Guam. "In essence," the IISS has hopefully concluded, "the military standoff that marked the end of the Korean War prevails."[40]

Confronted with very real prospects of a destructive military conflict on the peninsula that would lead to widespread regional instability, the United States and China have little choice but to engage in and coordinate painfully difficult regional and international diplomacy to convince Pyongyang to opt for the negotiating table over military confrontation. A key aspect of such diplomacy, however, will be China's propensity not to follow through in enforcing those sanctions against North Korea it has agreed to support in the United Nations (UN), and its role in pressuring the North to return to the Six Party Talks or other negotiations intended to denuclearize the Korean peninsula. As one analyst has correctly observed, "China, if it really wants to become a global leader, needs to pass this very critical litmus test."[41]

Sino-Japanese tensions over the Senkaku/Diaoyu Islands in the East China Sea have recently emerged as the other Northeast Asian flashpoint that could escalate out of control if not carefully managed. This territorial dispute escalated in September 2012 when the Japanese government purchased three of the main islands from their private (Japanese) owner in response to pressures by the nationalist governor of Tokyo to buy them if it declined to do so. The purchase offended China, which had long claimed ownership of this territory. It led to tense maneuvers between Chinese and Japanese air and naval units patrolling the area. The United States has acknowledged that its alliance commitments to Japan include defending its forces if they are attacked while defending Japan's administration of the islands. Washington has been equally clear, however, in resisting what many observers view to be the Abe government's excessively nationalist tendencies to challenge China's sovereign claims of Senkaku/Diaoyu.[42] Those claims reflect what China deems as its core interest in restoring its greatness by annexing what it regards as "lost territories." While hardly inclined to abandon Japan in the event China were to initiate overt military action to resolve this crisis in its favor, the United States equally wishes to avoid being entrapped into waging war over a Japanese ally's territorial dispute that falls short of constituting one of its own fundamental strategic interests.

This same posture has long shaped Washington's position toward territorial disputes in the South China Sea. China's claims for sovereign control over the Spratly Islands have positioned it at odds with rival claims by various ASEAN members. The United States insists that the UN Convention on the Law of the Sea allows it to conduct military exercises and operations in exclusive economic zones without coastal state notice or consent. China insists that such activities violate its domestic and international law. Future maritime incidents occurring directly between the United States and Chinese navies or resulting from China challenging the Philippines (a formal U.S. ally) in the contested territory could escalate into crises that would be increasingly hard to defuse.[43] Unlike the Cold War when the Soviet Union and the United States negotiated a series of confidence-building measures such as accidents-at-sea agreements, no commensurate dialogue mechanisms currently exist for Asia-Pacific maritime contingencies or locales. Effective initiatives are urgently required to clarify both when U.S. forces may be introduced to safeguard American interests in maintaining innocent passage through these waters—constituting one of the world's major trading lifelines—and to clarify the extent and limits of U.S. obligations to allies.

The United States and Multilateral Security in Asia.

Several forms of Asian multilateralism relate to the pivot strategy and overall U.S. strategic interests. Interactions involving regional navies engaging in joint exercises, confidence-building dialogues, and ship visits constitute a familiar kind of regional multilateralism that dovetails into the pivot strategy's broader vision of military diplomacy. As Assistant Secretary Campbell recently observed in a speech delivered in Sydney, the United States and China must become more instrumental in establishing rules of the road that would apply to future incidents or crises in ways designed to avoid conflict escalation. They must engage in such norm-building, however, as part of a multilateral process, involving ASEAN members and other relevant parties, and addressing such complex emerging issues as climate change and cyber security. Developing and strengthening habits of communication and predictability in response to widely observed norms often can be best facilitated within multilateral regional and international settings.[44] China's recent involvement in drawing up a sanctions package targeted toward its nominal ally, North Korea, within the UN Security Council framework is graphically illustrative.

Sustaining momentum for multilateral security initiatives will not be easy. China still harbors suspicions toward various multilateral military exercises that it regards as largely designed to contain its rising power. Chinese analysts have been especially critical of such exercises as the annual Cobra Gold multinational exercises co-hosted by Thailand and the United States and involving Vietnam, the Philippines, and Malaysia, which have territorial disputes with China. One Chinese naval expert has complained that while China has sent observers to Cobra Gold since 2002, the invitation for so many rival claimants to participate points to an American desire to generate bargaining chips that could be applied against China in the region over time. China, it is asserted, should host its own multilateral military exercises to counterbalance this perceived U.S. strategy.[45] China has also opposed many regional countries' preference for pursuing inclusive versions of multilateralism as represented by the East Asia Summit, which includes the United States as a member, preferring more Asian-centric models such as the ASEAN+3 configuration, which emerged in the aftermath of the 1997-98 Asian financial crisis.

Beijing's exclusivist orientation contradicts what many U.S. analysts believe to be a critical need for policy collaboration and resource sharing in the aftermath of a major regional crisis, such as a renewed Korean conflict. The U.S. Army War College's respected analyst Steven Metz has speculated that if such a war began "with out-of-the-blue North Korean missile strikes, China could conceivably even contribute to a multilateral operation to remove the Kim regime."[46] Bruce Bennett and Jennifer Lind's recent assessment of a government collapse in North Korea either through military defeat or internal implosion anticipates that complex military operations entailing postwar stabilization and humanitarian relief would be far-reaching in terms of global impact and potentially catastrophic implications:

> Perhaps the greatest danger is that countries will send their militaries in without coordination to stabilize the area or to secure the WMD. The specter of Chinese forces racing south while U.S. and South Korean troops race north is terrifying given the experience of the Korean War, a climate of suspicion among the three countries, and the risk of escalation to the nuclear level.[47]

Regional Trade and the Pivot Strategy.

The pivot strategy's three major themes—security, economy, and democracy—are intended to reinforce each other. It was therefore hardly coincidental that President Obama underscored the strategy's economic dimension by hosting the annual Asia-Pacific Economic Cooperation (APEC) forum in Honolulu in November 2011 just prior to highlighting the strategy's military and normative components in his speech to the Australian Parliament that same month. At the APEC meeting, Obama promoted the TPP, insisting that this initiative was gaining momentum. For it to acquire enduring significance, however, the TPP will need to fulfil a "mutually agreed prosperity" posture entailing Chinese participation on the basis of Sino-American economic interdependence. China would also need to recognize the legitimacy of the U.S. historic commercial and trading roles in the Asia-Pacific and the need for the region's smaller countries to "rebalance asymmetries" in their bilateral trade with China via TPP affiliation.[48] To date, however, Beijing has viewed the TPP as a hostile American effort to instill a containment policy through stealth that is directed toward China. Analysis provided by *Xinhua*, for example, observed that:

> The TPP, which pointedly excludes China, is widely seen as a thinly-disguised counterweight to free trade blocs in the region involving China and other Asian countries. In rare tough rhetoric, Obama also pointed a finger at China for not playing by the rules in trade and economic relations, pledging to 'continue to speak out and bring action' on issues such as currency and intellectual property rights.[49]

At an ASEAN summit in November 2012, China reaffirmed ASEAN+3 as its preferred vehicle for regional economic management. It begrudgingly accepted a twist to economic institution-building — complementing ASEAN+3 with a new regional grouping, the RCEP, initially comprised of ASEAN+3 members, India, Australia and New Zealand. RCEP's membership formula is inclusive (the United States and other states would be free to join once the organization's rules and infrastructure were in place). RCEP does not require the same degree of economic liberalization as does the TPP (in the areas of labor rights protection, environmental standards, reformed state-owned enterprises, intellectual property, and so on), affording China greater leeway to pursue bilateral trade and investment ties with its neighbors and distancing it from the imperatives for domestic economic and (by implication) political reform. Japan's recent interest in TPP affiliation, moreover, has obvious geo-economic implications for China. Embroiled in a major territorial dispute with Japan and apprehensive over what it perceives as the intensification of Japanese nationalism, China is less likely to view the TPP and RCEP as convergent paths to the same objective — a massive free-trade zone in Asia — than as competitive designs for organizing future Asian economic interaction.[50]

Promoting U.S. (and democratic allied) trading interests effectively relies on the U.S. ability to sustain regional influence and maintain a viable forward force presence in the Asia-Pacific. Such attributes provide necessary levels of breathing space needed to allow the complex process of regional economic organization to evolve and mature. U.S. military assets can be applied to a wide variety of traditional and nontraditional security contingencies that are relevant to preserving economic stability. The use of USPACOM augmentation teams to facilitate constructive regional engagement in humanitarian and disaster relief missions, for example, underscores U.S. use of Army, Marine Corps, and other military personnel to complement diplomatic and economic approaches for realizing and sustaining regional stabilization.[51]

RELATING THE PIVOT TO U.S. "EURASIAN" STRATEGY

A key question emanating from Washington's renewed strategic focus on Asia is how the pivot strategy will affect U.S. willingness and ability to maintain alliances and partnerships in Europe. The 2012 *Defense Strategic Guidance* statement acknowledged that the world's changing strategic landscape meant that the U.S. military posture toward Europe must evolve by adopting a "Smart Defense" approach to future Eurasian contingencies.[52] At the 49th Annual Munich Security conference convened in February 2013, Vice President Joe Biden nevertheless maintained that Europe remained the "cornerstone and catalyst for America's engagement with the world."[53] U.S. Deputy Secretary of Defense Ashton Carter emphasized U.S. determination to implement:

> approaches related to and aligned with the NATO Response Force concept of a highly ready and technologically advanced multinational force made up of land, air, maritime and special operations forces components that can quickly deploy.

In this context, Carter insisted the new U.S. defense strategy of rebalancing to the Asia-Pacific region is:

> not a rebalancing away from Europe because our interests are enduring here . . . . Europe is a source and not a consumer of security in today's world . . . and we look . . . to rebalance with Europe, not away from Europe.[54]

Citing President Obama's 2012 *Defense Strategic Guidance* as the operative framework, he stated that the United States would work with its European allies to research, acquire, and deploy cutting-edge technologies in such areas as special operations, intelligence, surveillance, reconnaissance, space, and cyberspace.

Despite this upbeat assessment and the relatively positive outcomes of recent NATO military operations in Libya, it remains unclear to what extent U.S. European allies will provide the levels of support that the 2012 *U.S. Defense Strategic Guidance* anticipated. In June 2011, U.S. Secretary of Defense Robert Gates castigated America's NATO partners over "shortages in military spending and political will" and warned that the alliance faced a "dim, if not dismal future" if the European member-states failed to increase their defense expenditures and responsibilities relative to U.S. spending and commitments.[55] Currently, NATO Europe spends on average about 1.6 percent gross domestic product (GDP) on defense (with Britain, France, and Germany comprising the vast bulk of this outlay—all other European members account for just 7.5 percent) and prospects are dim that this trend soon will be reversed.[56] That even the larger NATO allies would expend their resources to support the U.S. pivot strategy in Asia is even more remote, with at least some European policymakers reportedly aggrieved when the Obama administration first announced the *Guidance* initiative.[57] They have demonstrated much concern about the loss of sovereign control of military strategy and defense industrial jobs that the strategy implies.

Facing increased budgetary strain, U.S. policymakers have likewise adjusted U.S. force deployments in the NATO theater. Until recently, 88,000 of the 160,000 U.S. military personnel stationed overseas were deployed in Europe, while over half of all 50 U.S. bases located overseas (28) were on that continent. Recent studies by the RAND Corporation and the Congressional Budget Office estimated that ongoing U.S. Air Force and U.S. Army operations in Europe each cost around $1.7 billion annually.[58] The Obama administration has announced European theater force cuts of 11,000 personnel. These cuts will leave just under 70,000 U.S. military personnel in Europe, with initial reductions of basing operations in Germany and more such cuts on the way.[59] The United States has also delayed plans to deploy missile defense systems in Poland and Romania, and funding initially earmarked for that initiative will be directed to pay for ground based interceptor (GBI) systems to be deployed in Alaska. The latter is intended to defend against future North Korean and Iranian offensive missile systems capable of hitting U.S. targets.[60]

If the U.S. budget sequestration process evolves without resolution, U.S. power projection capabilities across Eurasia, along with traditional alliance objectives and missions, will clearly be affected. In the aftermath of the Iraq and Afghanistan wars, U.S. Landpower capabilities are particularly susceptible to budget reviews and requisite spending reductions.[61] These will not, however, be without restraint unless the United States decides that it will no longer be a global military power. Forward force deployments in Eurasia remain too cost-effective and geopolitically symbolic for that outcome to be acceptable to U.S. force planners. The American force presence in Europe directly supports U.S. strategic objectives in the Middle East, Afghanistan, and other extra-European or "out-of-area" theaters of operation. The U.S. Army's 21st Theater Sustainment Command operating out of Kaiserslautern, Germany, for example, provides critical logistical support for the U.S. Central Command which coordinates American military operations in the Middle East, Africa, and Central Asia. Over the past decade, around 75,000 U.S. Army Europe soldiers have deployed to Iraq and Afghanistan.[62]

Growing budgetary constraints, however, render both the geographic prioritization of American military resources and the conduct of efficient joint force operations inevitable. The pivot strategy anticipates that the greatest potential threats to U.S. national security interests will be state-centric challenges in Asia and extremist jihadist organizations in the Middle East, with strong prospects that the two types of threats could become increasingly linked over the next 2 decades. The U.S. Army has adopted *The Army Capstone Concept* (ACC) to ensure that it will fit seamlessly into the *Capstone Concept for Joint Operations: Joint Force 2020* designed to meet these two threats.[63] The ACC anticipates and justifies the Army's conversion from a force designed to fight and win two major wars simultaneously, to one that is expeditionary and does many things well. It assumes that most Army forces will be based in the United States but will deploy to overseas crises points when required.[64] The U.S. Army will need to be effective in an Asia-Pacific environment where seven of the world's 10 largest armies are operating in a highly dynamic and increasingly prosperous milieu, and in a Middle East where evolving democratic change relates directly to the democratization objectives that the pivot strategy is designed to promote. It must also adjust to allies' potential economic limitations in a prolonged global financial crisis. The NATO Smart Defense approach is just as applicable in a fluid Asia-Pacific strategic environment as it is to Europe.

Yet, there are clear anomalies between force planning and resource capabilities as underscored by shortfalls in both NATO's Smart Defense efforts and by USPACOM's Theater Campaign Plan (TCP). The TCP has recently been adjusted to operate on both an annual and 5-year basis in response to unanticipated military developments and to prospects of greater budget constraints. In testimony delivered to the House Armed Services Committee in March 2013, the Commander, USPACOM, warned that such constraints would impact negatively on USPACOM's ability to sustain lift capabilities so critical to a forward force presence and to engage systematically with regional allies and partners with respect to intensifying strategic risks.[65] A recent independent study conducted by the Center for Strategic and International Studies (CSIS) concluded that:

> There is a long history of inadequate resourcing for Combatant Command needs at the pre-conflict level of plans. Current processes to address that historical disconnect (such as the Integrated Priority Lists) are overwhelmed by other programmatic demands with higher dollar volumes.[66]

This problem will only intensify in a sequestration environment. More efficient country-level and regional-level force planning will need to be achieved between USPACOM and U.S. allies and partners. In regard to Landpower operating in USPACOM, the CSIS study recommends that the recent reassigning of I Corps and the 25th Infantry Divison from worldwide service rotation to permanent affiliation with USPACOM and the concentration of the III Marine Expeditionary Force on Pacific contingencies could well lead to greater efficiencies in joint training with allied forces and to more effective deployment patterns underpinning U.S. regional deterrence and defense strategies.[67] A test of such effectiveness would be to what extent current regional flashpoints can be contained from escalating into all-out conflicts that could tax American political will and material resources beyond acceptable risk.

CONCLUSION

Several overarching policy trends, as well as some specific implications for American Landpower, emerge from this analysis. Although re-balancing reflects a growing American recognition of Asia's seminal importance in the 21st century, it does not constitute a new U.S. grand strategy commensurate to the containment posture adopted during the Cold War. It instead represents a tactical effort to integrate military, economic, and diplomatic elements of U.S. policy into a broadly-based effort to reaffirm the U.S. presence and influence in the Pacific. The question remains, to what extent has that approach been understood by, and is acceptable to, the region's key players—most notably China. Most of America's traditional allies and many other regional countries have welcomed the pivot strategy as a geopolitical necessity to balance rising Chinese geopolitical clout. They have been restrained in endorsing it too openly lest their own increasingly substantial trading and politico-security relations with Beijing be compromised. China itself "is in no mood to support any U.S. pretensions to being the only, indispensable honest broker in the region."[68] Instead, it is pursuing its own vision of a regional order through strongly contesting its territorial claims in the East and South China Seas, opposing vigorously what it sees as

intensifying Japanese nationalism, lending only quali-
fied support to American-led efforts to contain North
Korea, and following a longer-term blueprint for pen-
etrating eventually the "first-island chain" — an arc of
archipelagos stretching from East Asia's continental
mainland coast to include Japan, Taiwan, the northern
Philipppines, Borneo, and the Malay Peninsula — in
ways required to preclude traditional U.S. dominance
in maritime East Asia. Without a gradual modification
in Chinese ambitions and behavior, and in the absence
of an highly nuanced U.S. diplomatic strategy combining a successful mix of engagement and cooperation with Beijing when Sino-American interests converge and a consistently firm and convincing posture
of competition when they do not, the pivot strategy
may ultimately be remembered as a catalyst for a new
Cold War in Asia.

A second policy concern confronting the pivot
strategy is whether regional security allies and partners in the Asia-Pacific will continue to support Washington's traditional bilateral security networks and
the centrality of U.S. force capabilities as the primary
means for sustaining an acceptable balance of power
in that region. Although the Obama administration
has explored multilateral security politics more extensively than its counterparts, it also views the bilateral
security network as the core element of its regional
security strategy. This remains true, notwithstanding
rebalancing's professed emphasis on greater outside-
bilateral alliance security partnerships. Examples of
this preference include: (1) Washington's recent up-
grading of rotational arrangements with Australia
and Singapore; (2) ongoing U.S. negotiations with
Japan over future basing arrangements in Okinawa,
while simultaneously acknowledging responsibili-

ties to defend Japan if it is attacked while defending its administrative control over the Senkaku/Diaoyu Islands area; (3) U.S. conditioning of South Korea's military to achieve an eventual transition of wartime command responsibilities in the event of renewed fighting on the Korean peninsula; and, (4) its careful calibration of policy responses to the Philippines' demands. All underscore the emphasis on the respective bilateral alliances.

Some plurilateral arrangements involving U.S. coordination with two allies simultaneously on various issues have been formed. The Trilateral Strategic Dialogue, involving Australia, Japan, and the United States, is one such arrangement. The Trilateral Coordination and Oversight Group was another. In neither case, however, has the initial momentum prompting the formation of such mechanisms been sustained. At the multilateral level, U.S. policymakers have identified specific crises such as an implosion of the North Korean regime where multilateral planning and cooperation could be applicable to restoring regional stability. These, however, are contingent on gaining intra-regional — and, above all, Chinese — consent.

For its own reasons, China actually appears to share the U.S. traditional skepticism about the value of multilateral security groupings as instruments for generating viable regional collective security arrangements that will simultaneously observe and safeguard great power interests. As a realist strategy oriented toward the balancing of regional power, the pivot strategy offers little in the way of guidelines for overcoming multilateralism's perceived weaknesses as an organizing principle for regional order-building.

U.S. and allied policy planners must overcome increasingly severe financial constraints on the pivot strategy. Not overcoming these constraints would effectively nullify the strategy. Such nullification would directly relate to how Landpower can fit and function in an increasingly fluid international power structure. It could require the U.S. Army and U.S. Marine Corp to make significant adjustments—and perhaps some major concessions—in the interest of fulfilling the "Joint Force 2020 Vision" outlined in the January 2012 *Defense Strategic Guidance* statement. That may entail those services reverting back to roles more in line with their long history, while relegating the pivot strategy's implementation largely to the U.S. Navy and Air Force and to U.S. Pacific allies. "Tomorrow's Army" may be charged with the defense of America and its allies safety by safeguarding the key Eurasian approaches and the island chains contiguous to U.S. territory. It could do so only by maintaining and refining a judicious combination of home-based and forward deployed combat elements, and by developing the requisite technologies needed for the United States to maintain its strategic edge over any power inclined to challenge America's key interests and values.

ENDNOTES - CHAPTER 1

1. Niall Ferguson, "A World Without Power," *Foreign Policy*, July 1, 2004, available from *www.foreignpolicy.com/articles/2004/07/01/a_world_without_power?page=0,3&wp_login_redirect=0*.

2. Zbigniew Brzezinski, "Giants, But Not Hegemons," *International Herald Tribune*, February 14, 2013; Kevin Rudd, "Beyond the Pivot: A New Roadmap for U.S.-Chinese Relations," *Foreign Affairs*, Vol. 92, No. 2, 2013, pp. 9-15.

3. Renowned American realist Stephen Walt reported in January 2013 that, at a conference of leading Chinese and American

thinkers on grand strategy convening in Beijing, there was a pre-vailing view that China and the United States would experience intense conflicts of interest in pursuing their respective grand strategies. Simply stated, China wants U.S. military power and economic influence marginalized, if not totally eliminated, in Asia in a manner reminiscent of the U.S. pursuit of the *Monroe Doctrine* in the 19th century, while America anticipates the need to retain U.S. power in Asia to preclude the Chinese domination of that continent. See Stephen Walt, "What I Told the Chinese," *Foreign Policy*, February 17, 2013, available from *walt.foreignpolicy.com/posts/2013/01/18/what_i_told_the_chinese*. The classic version of this perspective remains John Mearsheimer, *The Tragedy of Great Power Politics*, New York: Norton, 2001.

4. Office of the Press Secretary, "Remarks by President Obama to the Australian Parliament," Washington, DC: The White House, November 17, 2011, available from *www.whitehouse.gov/the-press-office/2011/11/17/remarks-president-obama-australian-parliament*.

5. U.S. Department of Defense, *Sustaining U.S. Global Leadership: Priorities for the 21st Century Defense*, Washington, DC: U.S. Government Printing Office (USGPO), January 2012, p. 2. Emphasis in the original document.

6. Thomas E. Donilon, as cited by Joseph S. Nye, Jr., "Work with China, Don't Contain It," *New York Times*, January 25, 2013, available from *www.nytimes.com/2013/01/26/opinion/work-with-china-dont-contain-it.html?*

7. A recent series presented by a Washington, DC, liberal think tank—the Foreign Policy Institute—in its *Foreign Policy in Focus* (FPIF) forum sharply criticizes the rationales and questions the feasibility of the strategy. Among other selections, see Joseph Gerson, "Reinforcing Washington's Asia-Pacific Hegemony," *FPIF*, September 13, 2012, available from *www.fpif.org/articles/reinforcing_washingtons_asia-pacific_hegemony*; Richard Javad Heydarian, "Raising the Stakes in Asia," *FPIF*, October 25, 2012, available from *www.fpif.org/articles/raising_the_stakes_in_asia*; Conn Hallinan, "Four More Years: The Asia Pivot," *FPIF*, December 26, 2012, available from *www.fpif.org/articles/four_more_years_the_asia_pivot*; and Winslow Wheeler, "Powering the Pacific 'Pivot,' with Leon and Chuck," *FPIF*, January 23, 2013, available from *www.fpif.org/articles/powering_the_pacific_pivot_with_leon_and_chuck*.

8. Craig Whitlock, "Philippines may allow greater U.S. military presence in reaction to China's rise," *New York Times*, January 26, 2012; Peter Drysdale, "America's Pivot to Asia and Asian Akrasia," *East Asia Forum*, November 26, 2012; Mark Thomson, "Australia's Response to U.S. Re-engagement in Asia: A Tale of Two Pivots," *East-West CenterVimeo*, September 25, 2012, available from *www.eastwestcenter.org/node/33780*.

9. Michael D. Swaine, "Chinese Leadership and Elite Responses to the U.S. Pacific Pivot," *China Leadership Monitor*, No. 38, August 6, 2012, available from *www.hoover.org/publications/china-leadership-monitor/9426*.

10. "The Geopolitics of the United States, Part I: The Inevitable Empire," *Stratfor Global Intelligence*, May 28, 2012, available from *www.stratfor.com/analysis/geopolitics-united-states-part-1-inevitable-empire*.

11. Steven Metz, "Strategic Horizons: Does America Need Two Armies?" *World Politics Review*, January 9, 2013, available from *www.worldpoliticsreview.com/articles/12612/strategic-horizons-does-america-need-two-armies*.

12. "The Geopolitics of the United States, Part 2: American Identity and the Threats of Tomorrow," *Stratfor Global Intelligence*, May 28, 2012, available from *www.stratfor.com/analysis/geopolitics-united-states-part-2-inevitable-empire*. However, Metz observes that, with the end of the Cold War, the U.S. Army became more expeditionary in response to the need to achieve quick deployments of decisive force and successful counterinsurgency campaigns rather than predominantly to undertake large-scale protracted war-fighting. See Metz, "Strategic Horizons: Does America Need Two Armies?"

13. Richard Fontaine and Kristin M. Lord, "Introduction: Debating America's Future," Richard Fontaine and Kristin M. Lord, eds., *America's Path: Grand Strategy for the Next Administration*, Washington, DC: Center for a New American Century, May 2012, p. 8.

14. Assistant Secretary Kurt M. Campbell, Bureau of East Asian and Pacific Affairs, Testimony before the House Committee of the Foreign Affairs Subcommittee on Asia and the Pacific, U.S. Department of State, Washington, DC, March 31, 2011, available from *www.state.gov/p/eap/rls/rm/2011/03/159450.htm*.

15. Dana H. Allin and Erik Jones, *Weary Policeman: American Power In An Age of Austerity*, International Institute for Strategic Studies, Oxford, UK: Routledge, 2012, pp. 167-168.

16. U.S. Forces Japan, Official Military Website, available from *www.usfj.mil/*.

17. National Institute for Defense Studies, Japan, *East Asian Strategic Review 2011, Japan Times*, Tokyo, Japan, 2011, pp. 252-256.

18. The recent *Yama Sakura* (December 2012) and Deployment Exercise (DEPEX—April 2013) maneuvers underscored the strengthening of logistical coordination between the GSDF and U.S. Army. See Kirk Spitzer, "U.S. Army to Asia: 'We're Back'," *Time*, December 7, 2012, available from *nation.time.com/2012/12/07/u-s-army-to-asia-were-back/*; and "U.S. Army and Japan hold first ever deployment exercise," *TX (Terminal X)*, April 30, 2013, available from *www.terminalx.org/2013/04/us-army-japan-hold-first-ever-depex.html*.

19. See Shaun Tandon, "Strong US, S. Korea Support for Alliance: Polls," October 15, 2012, available from *www.google.com/hostednews/afp/article/ALeqM5i7vGA2claNhtEoHEO20YOqQt0jww?docId=CNG.9c8ff903f2483b2a6a044cdbcbaf225b.941*; and Richard Weitz, "Global Insights: Obama-Lee Partnership Solidifies U.S.-South Korea Ties," *World Politics Review*, October 30, 2012, available from *www.worldpoliticsreview.com/articles/12459/global-insights-obama-lee-partnership-solidifies-u-s-south-korea-ties*.

20. South Korean analyst Chaesun Chung has recently observed that:

From a South Korean perspective, the long process of muddling through to find opportunities for strategic cooperation is very painful. Caught between the two countries [the U.S. and China], South Korea will suffer not only from an all-out confrontation but also from small, procedural disagreements based on strategic mistrust. More problematic for Seoul, as well as for many of the relatively weak countries neighboring China, is its lack of influence on the trajectory of U.S.-China relations.

Chaesun Chung, "U.S. Strategic Rebalancing to Asia: South Korea's Perspective," *Asia Policy*, Vol. 15, No. 1, 2013, p. 15.

21. Hugh White, "Caught in a Bind That Threatens An Asian War Nobody Wants," *Sydney Morning Herald*, December 26, 2012; and Rowan Callick, "Former PM Malcom Fraser's Speech on China and US Puts Him Out On 'The Fringe'," *The Australian*, September 27, 2012.

22. Peter Jennings, "The U.S. Rebalance to the Asia-Pacific: An Australian Perspective," *AsiaPolicy*, Vol. 15, No. 1, 2013, p. 42.

23. Charmaine G. Misalucha, "Southeast Asia-U.S. Relations: Hegemony or Hierarchy?" *Contemporary Southeast Asia*, Vol. 33, No. 2, 2011, p. 241.

24. "U.S. Military To Boost Philippines Presence; China Tells Army To Be Prepared," *Reuters*, December 12, 2012; "U.S. Secretary of State Hillary Clinton's Visit to the Philippines," *Asia Society (Australia)*, September 4, 2012, available from *asiasociety. org/australia/us-secretary-state-hillary-clinton%E2%80%99s-visit-philippines*.

25. Staff Sergeant Christopher McCullough, "US, Philippines partner for Exercise Balikatan," May 3, 2013, available from *www. army.mil/article/102588/US__Philippines_partner_for_Exercise_ Balikatan_2013/*.

26. Sasiwan Chingchit, "After Obama's Visit: The U.S.-Thailand Alliance and China," *Asia Pacific Bulletin* (East-West Center), No. 189, December 4, 2012, available from *www.eastwestcenter.org/ sites/default/files/private/apb189.pdf*.

27. U.S. Department of Defense, *Sustaining U.S. Global Leadership*, p. 2.

28. "Armies of India and US to hold wargames in September-October 2013," *TX*, May 25, 2013, available from *www.terminalx.org/2013/05/armies-of-india-us-to-hold-wargames-in-sept-oct-2013.html*.

29. Ajaya Kumar Das, *India-U.S. Maritime Partnership: Time to Move Forward*, RSIS Policy Brief, Singapore: S. Rajaratnam School of International Studies, August 2012, pp. 4, 7.

30. Robert Ayson, "Choosing Ahead of Time? Australia, New Zealand and the US-China Contest in Asia," *Contemporary Southeast Asia*, Vol. 34, No. 3, 2012, pp. 345-347.

31. "NZDF, Australia and US Conduct Exercise Alam Hafa 2013," *army-technology.com*, May 10, 2013, available from *www.army-technology.com/news/newsnzdf-australia-and-us-conduct-exercise-alam-halfa-2013*; and Bruce Vaughn, *New Zealand: Background and Bilateral Relations with the United States*, CRS 7-5700, Washington, DC: USGPO, May 27, 2011, pp. 9-10.

32. Tim Huxley, "Singapore and the US: Not Quite Allies," *The Strategist* (Australian Strategic Policy Institute Blog), July 2012, available from *www.aspistrategist.org.au/author/tim-huxley/*.

33. Sergeant Robert M. England, "Hawaii Soldiers welcome Singapore Army, prepare for Tiger Balm 2012," *www.army.mil*, July 11, 2012, available from *www.army.mil/article/83359/Hawaii_Soldiers_welcome_Singapore_Army__prepare_for_Tiger_Balm_2012/*.

34. Das, *India-U.S. Maritime Partnership*, pp. 3-4; "India and America: Less than Allies, More Than Friends," *Economist*, June 16, 2012, available from *www.economist.com/node/21556935*.

35. Gary Hawke, "Is New Zealand Trapped in the Anglosphere?" *East Asia Forum*, January 18, 2013, available from *www.eastasiaforum.org/2013/01/18/new-zealand-stayed-insular-in-2012/*.

36. Huxley.

37. Rudd.

38. Brendan P. O'Reilly, "Pivot Could Cost Obama, Asia Dearly," *Asia Times Online*, January 30, 2013, available from *www.atimes.com/atimes/China/OA30Ad01.html*.

39. International Institute for Strategic Studies (IISS), *The Military Balance 2011*, Oxford, UK: Routledge, 2011, p. 206.

40. IISS, *North Korea's Weapons Programs: A Net Assessment,* January 21, 2004, available from *www.iiss.org/publications/strategic-dossiers/north-korean-dossier/.*

41. Interview with Jung-Hoon Lee, former South Korean national security adviser and Professor of International Relations, Yonsei University, Seoul, Korea, *Radio Australia*, March 11, 2013, available from *www.radioaustralia.net.au/international/radio/program/connect-asia/north-korea-threatens-war-over-un-sanctions/1099812.*

42. See Yoshihide Soeya, "How Can Japan Navigate the Senkaku Dispute and China's Rise?" *East Asia Forum*, March 10, 2013, available from *www.eastasiaforum.org/2013/03/10/how-can-japan-navigate-the-senkaku-dispute-and-chinas-rise/.*

43. Bonnie S. Glaser, "Armed Clash in the South China Sea," *Council on Foreign Relations Contingency Memorandum No. 14*, April 2012, available from *www.cfr.org/east-asia/armed-clash-south-china-sea/p27883.*

44. Kurt Campbell, "Alliance 21 Emerging Asia Address: The United States, China and Australia," Customs House, Sydney, Australia, March 14, 2013, available from *alliance21.org.au/events/Kurt-Campbell-Address. Also see Rory Medcalf, "Can Military Diplomacy Keep the Peace in 2013?" *The Diplomat,* January 5, 2013, available from *thediplomat.com/flashpoints-blog/2013/01/05/can-military-diplomacy-keep-the-peace-in-2013/.*

45. Citing comments by Beijing naval expert Li Jie, "Experts say drills stir up disputes," *Stratrisks*, February 8, 2012, available from *stratrisks.com/geostrat/3924. Also see "Repressing China: Multilateral Exercise Cobra Gold Takes On a New Look," *Stratrisks*, February 13, 2013, available from *stratrisks.com/geostrat/10795.*

46. Steven Metz, "Strategic Horizons: Thinking the Unthinkable on a Second Korean War," *World Politics Review*, March 13, 2013, available from *www.worldpoliticsreview.com/articles/12786/strategic-horizons-thinking-the-unthinkable-on-a-second-korean-war.*

47. Bruce W. Bennett and Jennifer Lind, "The Collapse of North Korea: Military Missions and Requirements," *International Security*, Vol. 36, No. 2, 2011, p. 85.

48. Patrick Mendis, "How Washington's Asia Pivot and the TPP Can Benefit Sino-American Relations," *East Asia Forum*, March 6, 2013, available from *www.eastasiaforum.org/2013/03/06/ how-washingtons-asia-pivot-and-the-tpp-can-benefit-sino-american-relations/*.

49. Zhi Linfei and Ran Wei, "Yearender: Obama Administration's Pivot Strategy Sows More Seeds of Suspicion Than Cooperation," *Xinhua*, December 23, 2011, available from *news.xinhuanet. com/english/indepth/2011-12/23/c_131323762.htm*.

50. Donald Emmerson, "Challenging ASEAN: The American Pivot in Southeast Asia," *East Asia Forum*, January 13, 2013, available from *www.eastasiaforum.org/2013/01/13/challenging-asean-the-american-pivot-in-southeast-asia/*.

51. See, for example, Donna Miles, "Pacom Exercise Program Integrates Disaster Response Preparation," *Defense.gov News*, September 5, 2012, available from *www.defense.gov/news/newsarticle. aspx?id=117750*.

52. U.S. Department of Defense, *Sustaining U.S. Global Leadership*, p. 3.

53. Jim Garamone, "Europe Remains Cornerstone Of U.S. Engagement, Biden Says," *U.S. Army Europe*, February 5, 2013, available from *www.eur.army.mil/news/2013/20130205_Biden_Munich.html*.

54. Cheryrl Pellerin, "Partners Essential in Strategic Transition, Carter Says," *Defense.gov*, February 2, 2013, available from *www.defense.gov/news/newsarticle.aspx?id=119180*.

55. Thom Shanker, "Defense Secretary Warns NATO of 'Dim' Future," *New York Times*, June 10, 2011.

56. Doug Bandow, "The Continent Without a Military," *The National Interest*, February 25, 2013, available from *nationalinterest. org/commentary/the-continent-without-military-8152?page=1*.

57. Anna Mulrine, "In Pentagon's 'Pivot' Toward Asia, Has Europe Been Forgotten?" *Christian Science Monitor*, November 2012.

58. Cited by Adam Grissom, "The United States," Clara Marina O'Donnell, ed., *The Implications of Military Spending Cuts for NATO's Largest Members*, Washington, DC: Brookings Institution, July 2012, p. 26.

59. *Ibid.*, p. 25.

60. "U.S. Axes Europe Missile Defence Interceptor," *news com.au*, March 16, 2013, available from *www.news.com.au/breaking-news/world/us-axes-europe-missile-defence-interceptor/story-e6fr-fkui-1226598768407*.

61. Thomas P. M. Barnett notes that the U.S. Army and Marine Corps were the primary beneficiaries of "supplemental" U.S. defense expenditures in the post 9/11 era, while the Navy and Air Force allocation of the total defense budget declined by several percentage points. Accordingly, "[i]ncluding two land wars that enlarged his two armies—the Army and Marine Corps—the president can reduce their superexpensive manpower." Thomas P. M. Barnett, "Think Again: The Pentagon," *Foreign Policy*, March/April 2013, available from *www.foreignpolicy.com/articles/2013/03/04/the_pentagon?page=0,1*.

62. Luke Coffey, "Keeping America Safe: Why U.S. Bases in Europe Remain Vital," Heritage Foundation Special Report # 111, Washington, DC: Heritage Foundation, July 11, 2012, available from *www.heritage.org/research/reports/2012/07/keeping-america-safe-why-us-bases-in-europe-remain-vital*.

63. Department of the Army, *U.S. Training and Doctrine Command Pamphlet 525-3-0, The U.S. Army Capstone Concept*, Washington, DC: USGPO, December 19, 2012, pp. 4-5.

64. *Ibid.*, p. 5.

65. "Statement of Admiral Samuel J. Locklear, U.S. Navy, Commander, U.S. Pacific Command on U.S. Pacific Command Posture," Armed Services Committee, U.S. House of Representatives, Washington, DC, March 5, 2013, available from *www.pacom.mil/documents/pdf/20130305-hasc-adm-locklear-posture-statement.pdf.*

66. David Berteau and Michael J. Green, Co-Directors, *U.S. Force Posture Strategy in the Asia-Pacific Region: An Independent Assessment,* Washington, DC: Center for Strategic and International Studies, August 2012, p. 90.

67. *Ibid.,* pp. 92-93; "Statement of Admiral Samuel J. Locklear," pp. 30-31.

68. Peter Lee, "US Learns Hard Lessons Of 'Asia Pivot'," *Asia Times Online,* October 27, 2012, available from *www.atimes.com/atimes/China/NJ27Ad01.html.*

CHAPTER 2

MILITARY SOFT POWER IN THE 21ST CENTURY: MILITARY EXCHANGES AND PARTNER DEVELOPMENT

Carol Atkinson

In the 21st century, success in the conduct of military missions will depend more than ever on the effective integration of hard and soft power, or what has been called smart power. For the U.S. Armed Forces, military smart power entails the integrated use of military capabilities with the ability to co-opt, persuade, and influence the thinking of others. Much has been written on the harder aspects of military power; in contrast, this article will focus on its softer side, or what might be called **military soft power**.[1]

One important and effective strategy to build military soft power is through the military educational exchange programs hosted by U.S. war and staff colleges. These programs help the United States to build partnerships with potential coalition nations that enhance not only U.S. national security but also international peace and stability. The exchanges help the United States to extend its influence or military soft power through international networks of military professionals. This chapter will examine the importance of these exchanges. First, the chapter lays out some broad ideas about the nature of military power, specifically how we might think about military soft power. Second, the chapter will focus on the important role that educational exchanges sponsored by the U.S. military play in building military soft power and how the United States might improve its capabilities to do this. However, before delving more deeply into theory, it would be instructive to begin with what happened in one of the greatest empires in world history, the Mongols under Genghis Khan. The methods used by the Mongols to conquer and administer their empire illustrate several important lessons about the nature of power that remain relevant for us today.

In the 13th century, the warriors of Genghis Khan swept across Asia, the Middle East, and Eastern Europe, easily defeating the armies they encountered. At the time of Genghis Khan's reign, the Mongol army consisted of only around 100,000 warriors from a total Mongol population of 700,000 to one million.[2] The Mongol's empire, however, would eventually extend from Korea to Eastern Europe, encompassing modern day China, Russia, and Iran. With so few men, brute force coercion could never have won the empire, nor held it together.

In order to hold their empire together, the Mongols needed to co-opt and incorporate other nations to become partners in the administration and defense of the empire. In so doing, the accomplishments of the Mongols were staggering. Within their empire, the Mongol rulers built political institutions based on promotion by merit rather than aristocratic birth; established the world's largest free trade zone; created an international legal regime that established rule of law that applied equally to commoners and rulers; abolished torture; encouraged religious freedom and toleration; established a regular census; introduced a universal alphabet; began universal education for all children; introduced paper currency; established a transcontinental postal service; and created what we recognize today as the modern states of Russia and China.[3] In thinking about the many institutions built by the Mongols to administer and manage their empire, parallels to U.S. accomplishments in both Europe and Asia after World War II come to mind.

The list of accomplishments of the Mongol empire might be surprising to many people. The reason that the achievements of the *Pax Mongolica* are not well known is because western histories have focused on the brutal aspects of the empire in Europe rather than its many accomplishments from Persia to China.[4] Contrary to Western histories that have focused almost exclusively on the hard power aspects of Mongol rule, the Mongols were able to build the largest empire in human history and administer it because of their synergistic use of both hard and soft power, or what Joseph Nye has called smart power.[5] In advice that still rings true today, Genghis Khan told his sons: "Conquering an army is not the same as conquering a nation. You may conquer an army with superior tactics and men, but you can conquer a nation only by conquering the hearts of the people."[6]

But what exactly are hard power and soft power — and how can we distinguish between them? Hard power is the ability to get others to act contrary to their own desires and preferences usually through the use of threats and incentives. So, for example, while a country's leaders might prefer to rule their people through autocratic means, the United States might use military threats or economic sanctions to coerce autocratic leaders to improve their human rights practices or to permit greater freedoms for their people. In the use of military hard power, the dictators' preferences to rule autocratically have not been changed; only their behavior has changed. In the starkest cases, such as Iraq, military hard power can be used to impose a new system of government.

Soft power, on the other hand, is the ability to change someone's values, beliefs, and preferences. The successful use of soft power results in a change in preferences that subsequently affects behavior. Because the person's beliefs and preferences were altered, it is very unlikely he would revert to his old behavior because that behavior was based on preferences that he no longer holds. Soft power is the co-option of others through agenda setting, persuasion, and attraction.[7] Unlike the use of hard power, the recipient of the effects of soft power may not even be aware of what is happening.[8] Soft power can be built through the actions of government agents; for example, by pursuing public diplomacy strategies that engage foreign publics.[9] These diplomatic actions include holding town meetings, giving interviews, organizing outreach programs, sponsoring international exchanges, and managing virtual communications.[10] Soft power can also be gained through what Nye called structural effects, meaning setting an example that others wish to emulate—in short to serve as the "shining city on the hill."[11] Merging these two mechanisms, we can also think about how a country's soft power can be built by nongovernmental agents through the transmission of a country's popular culture in the form of movies, music, fashion, food, and even video games. In sum, a country exerts soft power on others through its culture, values, and policies. Soft power accrues to the entity whose culture is pleasing to others; whose values are attractive and consistently practiced; and whose policies are seen as inclusive and legitimate.[12]

Military soft power might be an odd concept to some people, because soft power is usually ascribed to diplomatic efforts conducted by the U.S. State Department. The U.S. military, on the other hand, is usually associated with hard power. However, the U.S. military is in a position to wield a tremendous amount of soft power because its culture, values, and policies are held in high esteem both within the United States and within the armed forces of many countries around the world.[13]

The U.S. Armed Forces are certainly a lot bigger than the Mongol army, but a similar situation faces the United States today as was faced by the Mongol rulers. The difficulties of relying too much on hard power were illustrated in the early years of the recent U.S. wars in Iraq and Afghanistan. Additionally, several trends in international politics make the use of hard power, especially, military hard power, problematic for the United States. First, there has been a tremendous increase in the number of democratic governments worldwide. Today, there are over four times as many democracies in the world as there are dictatorships.[14] If we take the democratic peace theory[15] to heart, this also means that there are far fewer situations where the United States would choose to use its military hard power to resolve a dispute. Second, since the end of the Cold War, there has been a dramatic decline in major armed conflict both in terms of the number of countries affected and in terms of total magnitude; both interstate warfare and civil warfare have declined substantially.[16] Third, scholars such as John Mueller have argued that warfare as we knew it in the 20th century as a battle between disciplined military forces will be replaced by policing wars. The function of U.S. armed forces will be to put terrorists, thugs, and criminals that have become too powerful for police forces, back into their place. According to Mueller, the new policing wars will never eliminate the threat but only subdue it to a tolerable level.[17] Thus, there will always be policing activities to contend with.

Within this international context, the U.S. Department of Defense (DoD) has identified declining U.S. budgets, a shift in U.S. strategic emphasis to Asia-Pacific, and a broadening focus on policing types of activities as key trends that the U.S. Army of the early 21st century will need to consider.[18] The 2012 DoD *Strategic Guidance* is quite clear in defining the primary missions of the U.S. Armed Forces: counter-terrorism and irregular warfare; deter and defeat aggression; project power despite anti-access/area denial challenges; counter weapons of mass destruction; operate effectively in cyberspace and space; maintain a safe, secure, and effective nuclear deterrent; defend the homeland and provide support of civil authorities; provide a stabilizing presence; conduct stability and counterinsurgency operations; and conduct humanitarian, disaster relief, and other operations.[19] Most of these missions would be difficult to accomplish through the use of hard power only. For noncombat missions, military soft power assets are likely to be key such as in working with partner nations to provide a stabilizing presence. Military soft power can also enhance the ability of the United States and its partner nations when the use of coercive military force might be necessary such as in missions to project power and to conduct counter-terrorism operations.

Partner nations will play an important role as the U.S. military transitions to address these priorities. U.S. Army Chief of Staff Raymond Odierno has emphasized that, "as we shift away from active involvement in major combat operations, we will increasingly emphasize activities aimed at deepening out relationships with partners."[20] The 2012 *Defense Strategic*

Guidance also reminded us that building partnerships remains important for sharing the costs and responsibilities of global leadership.[21] The emphasis on partnerships is certainly evident in a rather astounding doctrinal change for the U.S. Air Force that now considers "building partnerships" a core mission, equivalent to its foundational mission of gaining and maintaining air superiority. Thus, in the emerging international politics of the 21st century, building and sustaining partnerships will be a key task for military leaders. Partnerships rely on soft power, and it behooves all of us to think about how we as strategists, policymakers, and practitioners might build military soft power as a complement to military hard power and an important source of influence in its own right.

One way to build soft power is through exchange programs. Centuries ago, Genghis Khan recognized the importance of exchanges as a way to build his own warriors' expertise and knowledge. The Mongols organized and patronized exchanges of personnel in order to build more effective ruling institutions as well as to further commerce and bring wealth and knowledge to their people.[22] Indeed, military personnel exchanges were important and extensively conducted within the Mongol empire between its eastern reaches in what is now China with its western reaches in what is now Iran, the Middle East, and Europe. German artillerymen and soldiers from Greece, Russia, Scandinavia, Arabia, and Persia could be found in the eastern reaches of the Mongol empire; whereas Uighur, Kitan, Tibetan, and Chinese soldiers were exchanged into the western areas of the empire.[23] Each brought their expertise and experience to their new units.

One very important way the U.S. military builds soft power is through U.S.-hosted military educational exchange programs.[24] Successive U.S. secretaries of state have all heralded student exchange programs as a powerful source of soft power.[25] Military exchange programs at U.S. war and staff colleges are very influential because they impact people who are likely to be in elite leadership positions within their countries. For the United States, the goal of the military exchanges is multi-faceted. Certainly, they help to build relationships with other militaries that can improve the effectiveness of multinational operations. Just as important, the exchanges serve as a source of information for international participants about military topics as well as about the United States, its people, and its values. Likewise, the international participants bring new perspectives to share with their U.S. counterparts. When the exchange officers' experiences in the United States are positive, the exchanges help the United States to extend its influence through **soft** rather than **hard** power.

The International Military Education and Training program (IMET) is the U.S. military's premier exchange program. It is funded by the State Department, but run by the DoD. IMET programs are extensive and varied; they are also relatively inexpensive. On an annual basis, IMET funds about 7,000 foreign military and civilian personnel from about 140 countries to receive training in more than 4,000 formal courses at approximately 150 U.S. military schools and installations for a total cost of around $97 million dollars[26] or about 0.2 percent of the State Department budget. IMET funds many of the international officers who attend the courses at U.S. war and staff colleges. The presence of foreign military officers at U.S. elite military schools, its war and staff colleges, is substantial. Approximately 10-20 percent of the student bodies at

U.S. war and staff colleges are international officers. The U.S. Army's Command and General Staff College (CGSC) has the longest running program, hosting international officers since 1894.[27] As of 2012, more than 7,300 foreign military officers had graduated from the CGSC. Of these, more than half had obtained the rank of general, and 250 officers from 69 different countries had become heads of their militaries or heads of state. Of these, 28 international graduates of the CGSC have become heads of states.[28] In 2005, Indonesian President Susilo Bambang Yudhoyono, a former military officer and 1991 graduate of the CGSC, became the first sitting head of state to be inducted into the CGSC alumni hall of fame. Yudhoyono was widely credited with bringing peaceful democratic transition to his country. At the more senior level, the U.S. Army War College (USAWC) graduated its first international students in 1978. Since those early years, the number of international fellows has steadily increased. It is impressive to note that 18 international alumni from this one school alone are currently serving as army or defense chief in their countries — Germany, Korea, India, Canada, Denmark, Uganda, Norway, Egypt, Italy, Philippines, Lithuania, New Zealand, Oman, Australia, Hungary, Estonia, Georgia, and the Netherlands.[29] Approximately, 10 percent of all international alumni of the USAWC become army or defense chiefs in their respective countries.[30]

U.S.-hosted military exchanges at U.S. war and staff colleges are important venues where military officers from different countries build social and professional networks. The friendships and professional contacts between foreign officers studying in the United States and their U.S. counterparts help to improve the ability of the U.S. military to work with allied nations as well as potential coalition partners. In addition, these personal and professional military networks can support the development of democratic norms and practices in countries where these institutions are underdeveloped. As anthropologist Margaret Mead pointed out: "Democratic procedures are not something that people have, like automobiles or hot-dog stands or a way of building roads" — it is a way of behaving and an attitude of mind that must be nurtured by society.[31] Hosting military personnel from less than democratic countries is one important way to build the knowledge and experience necessary for people to build and sustain democratic institutions and practices.

Building military soft power is a process that takes place over numerous years, even decades, during which both the beliefs of individuals and the ideas espoused by their military communities are mutually constituted through multiple interactions. This makes the study of soft power difficult, as results are not immediate and are difficult to measure. Nevertheless, results do occur as is evident by the many anecdotes told by U.S. officers and their international colleagues about their continuing friendships and interactions that occur in the years following their graduation from a U.S. war or staff college.

Systematic empirical measurement of the long-term impact of military-to-military exchanges is difficult, but not impossible. Data indicate that the officers who come to school in the United States are likely to reach positions of power in their home countries. As already noted, there are hundreds of graduates who have highly influential military and political positions. In response to my surveys of the U.S. military institution graduating classes in 2010, 80 percent of the international officers said that they were returning to jobs with more responsibility after their year abroad in the United States.[32] Sixty-five percent of them knew of previous graduates in their home country who now held "very important military jobs."[33] This is signifi-cant, because it means that there are cohorts of mili-tary officers in countries around the world who spent a year abroad in the United States, who likely have fond memories of those times and the friends they made. These graduates know each other, and keep in contact with their military colleagues abroad. When asked to reflect upon the most important thing they learned about the United States during their time at a U.S. war or staff college, international participants identify aspects of how Americans think and act, how U.S. democracy works, and different aspects about U.S. lifestyles and culture rather than information about U.S. military operations, doctrine, or strategy. Thus, an important function of war and staff colleges is not necessarily imparting factual historical or doctrinal information, but rather providing the environment in terms of cultural, social, and personal interactions that builds social networks and positive perceptions of the United States. Indeed, the international exchanges do just that. The international officers identify that the best aspects of America are (in order to precedence): 1) the U.S. people and U.S. culture, 2) governance and rule of law in the United States, 3) freedom, 4) democ-racy, and 5) opportunities.[34] This is not to say that all impressions are positive. When asked what the United States should improve, the international officers iden-tified (in order to precedence): 1) U.S. knowledge of the rest of the world, 2) U.S. respect for other cultures, and 3) U.S. foreign relations.[35] Much like exchange students the world over, most of the officers return home with positive impressions of the United States and hope to remain in contact with their classmates from the United States and other countries.

These findings suggest at least two important policy implications. First, military educational exchanges are an important tool of U.S. diplomatic engagement. As former Secretary of State Hillary Clinton argued: "[T]he durability of the United States' partnerships abroad will depend on the attitudes of the people as well as the policies of their governments."[36] It is not wise to use these programs in a carrot-and-stick manner. In fact, denying school slots as a punishment for bad behavior, such as a nation's human rights abuses, undermines the ability of the United States to extend its influence within the political and military hierarchies of those countries, and in the longer term change this bad behavior by changing the preferences of the leadership, rather than just temporarily changing their outward behavior through force or pressure. Second, providing financial support so that officers can bring their families with them is a very important way that the United States could build a tremendous amount of good will for a relatively trivial amount of money. Already, most of the officers bring their spouses and families with them on their exchange program, but some cannot afford to do so. These officers are likely to come from regions of the world in which the United States would like to extend its soft power: Central Asia and Africa.

Within military circles, exchange programs such as those discussed previously and the attendant benefits of the social networks that they build are generally well known. However, outside of the military, there is considerably less knowledge about the existence of these programs and their importance not only to U.S. national security, but also to international security in the 21st century. Military exchange students are much like exchange participants the world over — they generally return home with warm feelings toward their host nation and the people that they met. They share their experiences with friends and family, and they hope to remain in contact with the people they met during their exchange program. Through these programs, the United States can build its influence over the longer term. At the same time, much like the Mongol warriors, U.S. officers can learn new ways of doing things and new perspectives that enhance the U.S. ability to work with partner nations and, when necessary, use its hard power assets.

ENDNOTES - CHAPTER 2

1. Carol Atkinson, *Military Soft Power*, book manuscript, 2013.

2. Jack Weatherford, *Genghis Khan and the Making of the Modern World*, New York: Three Rivers Press, 2004, p. xviii; Thomas T. Allsen, *Culture and Conquest in Mongol Eurasia*, Cambridge, UK: Cambridge University Press, 2001, p. 5.

3. Weatherford.

4. Allsen, p. 5. It has only been since the discovery and translation of the *Secret History of the Mongols* in the 20th century that a more balanced historical narrative has begun to emerge.

5. Joseph S. Nye, Jr., *The Future of Power*, New York: Public Affairs, 2011, pp. 22-23.

6. As retold in Weatherford, p. 125.

7. Nye, *The Future of Power*, p. 16.

8. *Ibid.*, p. 14.

9. *Ibid.*, p. 17.

10. Hillary Rodham Clinton, "Leading Through Civilian Power: Redefining American Diplomacy and Development," *Foreign Affairs*, Vol. 89, No. 6, 2010, pp. 13-24.

11. Nye, *The Future of Power*, p. 17.

12. Joseph S. Nye, Jr., "Get Smart: Combining Hard and Soft Power," *Foreign Affairs,* Vol. 88, No. 4, 2009, p. 161.

13. U.S. citizens have consistently rated the U.S. military as the U.S. institution in which they have the most confidence. For example, see the Harris Poll, "Current Confidence in Leaders of Institutions," Harris Poll #44, May 21, 2012. The poll is available from *www.harrisinteractive.com*. In this 2012 poll, 55 percent of people expressed a "great deal" of confidence in U.S. military leaders. Comparable figures were 27 percent for the Supreme Court, 23 percent for organized religion, 22 percent for the White House, 11 percent for the press, and 6 percent for Congress.

14. As of late 2011, the Polity IV Project rated 95 countries as full democracies and only 22 countries as full autocracies. See Monty G. Marshall and Benjamin R. Cole, *Global Report 2011: Conflict, Governance, and State Fragility*, Vienna, VA: Center for Systemic Peace, 2011. Their report is available from *www.systemicpeace.org/GlobalReport2011.pdf*.

15. The democratic peace theory holds that democracies rarely, if ever, engage in armed disputes with each other.

16. Marshall and Cole, pp. 3-4.

17. John Mueller, *The Remnants of War*, Ithaca, NY: Cornell University Press, 2004.

18. Raymond Odierno, "The Army in a Time of Transition," *Foreign Affairs*, Vol. 91, No. 3, 2012, pp. 7-11; U.S. Department of Defense, *Sustaining U.S. Global Leadership: Priorities for the 21st Century Defense*, Washington, DC, Department of Defense, January, 2012.

19. U.S. Department of Defense, pp. 4-6.

20. Odierno, p. 11.

21. U.S. Department of Defense, p. 3.

22. Allsen, pp. 193-199.

23. Allsen, p. 6.

24. Carol Atkinson, "Does Soft Power Matter? A Comparative Analysis of Student Exchange Programs, 1980-2006," *Foreign Policy Analysis*, Vol. 6, No. 1, 2010, pp. 1-22; Carol Atkinson, "Constructivist Implications of Material Power: Military Engagement and the Socialization of States, 1972-2000," *International Studies Quarterly*, Vol. 50, No. 3, pp. 509- 537.

25. John Kerry, "Secretary of State Kerry Highlights Exchange Programs in First Official Speech," Address to the University of Virginia, February 20, 2013; Clinton, pp. 13-24; Condoleezza Rice, "Remarks at the U.S. University Presidents Summit on International Education Dinner," Washington, DC, January 5, 2006.

26. U.S. Department of Defense and U.S. Department of State, *Foreign Military Training, Fiscal Years 2010 and 2011*, Joint Report to Congress, Vol. I, Washington, DC: Department of Defense and Department of State, 2011, p. II-2.

27. John Reichley, *International Officers: A Century of Participation at the United States Army Command and General Staff College*, Fort Leavenworth, KS: U.S. Army Command and General Staff College, 1994.

28. Harry Sarles, "CGSC inducts new International Hall of Fame members," *www.army.mil*, April 25, 2013, available from *www.army.mil/article/101944/CGSC_inducts_new_International_Hall_of_Fame_members/*.

29. John Burbank, "German, Dutch Army Chiefs Inducted into Hall of Fame," *The Torch*, Spring 2013, p. 25.

30. *Ibid.*, p. 25.

31. Margaret Mead, *And Keep Your Powder Dry: An Anthropologist Looks At America*, New York: William Morrow and Company, 1942, p. 20.

32. Atkinson, *Military Soft Power.*

33. *Ibid.*

34. *Ibid.*

35. *Ibid.*

36. Clinton, p. 16.

CHAPTER 3

REBALANCING AND THE ROLE OF ALLIES AND PARTNERS: EUROPE, NATO, AND THE FUTURE OF AMERICAN LANDPOWER

Sean Kay

> . . . we don't need to send tens of thousands of our sons and daughters abroad, or occupy other nations. Instead, we will need to help countries like Yemen, Libya, and Somalia provide for their own security, and help allies who take the fight to terrorists, as we have in Mali.
>
> President Barack Obama,
> State of the Union Address,
> February 2013.

INTRODUCTION AND OVERVIEW

Dramatic cuts in overseas Landpower presence in Europe can combine smart strategy with budget priorities that can incentivize allies and partners to better coordinate for their own security provision. If done well with a clear plan, then a much larger realignment of American forces out of Europe will allow for either cost savings by decommissioning elements, or protecting against a hollow force in key areas of the world, driven by deepening budget cuts to the U.S. Army and other land forces. Europe is the proper place to save money and realign resources toward areas of greater priority for overseas deployments. Geopolitical, budgetary, and political trends are leading to major U.S. land forces reductions in Europe. Missing, however, is a strategic rationale. By limiting America's role in the

North Atlantic Treaty Organization (NATO) to collective defense and working with allies and partners to enable them to engage in European area military operations without the United States, a new transatlantic security architecture can be achieved. Combined with a new prioritization of transatlantic trade, the U.S.-European alliance can be made more durable and relevant to contemporary challenges. Failure to align military cuts with strategic goals risks further erosion of the transatlantic security architecture and misses an opportunity to gain more operational capacity from America's allies and partners.

GLOBAL SECURITY AND STRATEGIC REBALANCING OF LANDPOWER

The global security environment of the early 21st century offers a window for the United States to change incentives and promote better integrated capabilities among allies and partners. By 2010, the United States based over 160,000 peacetime personnel overseas. Over half of that deployment was in Europe.[1] The risk of general war in Europe, however, is lower than at any point in contemporary history. While there are peripheral challenges near to the European area, these can and should be handled by America's European allies and partners working within NATO. The drawdown from Cold War levels of several hundred thousand American land forces in Europe over the last 20 years has, however, not prompted allies and partners to offset capabilities to pursue independent action. Additionally, the United States no longer needs Europe as an essential perch to project military power for global security interests as it did in the 1990-91 Persian Gulf crisis. Meanwhile, wars in Iraq and Afghanistan have taken a toll on policymakers and public attitudes about future land wars. As former Secretary of Defense Robert Gates said to a West Point audience in early 2011:

> In my opinion, any future defense secretary who advises the president to again send a big American land army into Asia or into the Middle East or Africa should have his head examined. . . . As the prospects for another head-on clash of large mechanized land armies seem less likely, the Army will be increasingly challenged to justify the number, size, and cost of its heavy formations.[2]

While the conditions are not good for a departure of American capabilities from the Persian Gulf, the need to bolster them, shift focus toward Asia, and save money provide a rationale for removing almost all U.S. land forces presence from Europe.[3]

As President Barack Obama suggested in his February 2013 State of the Union address, fighting terrorists and other asymmetrical threats does not require tens of thousands of troops deployed to foreign lands. Moreover, emerging security challenges such as population and demographic pressures, democracy and human rights, transnational diseases, environmental and energy security, and cyber security are not amenable to large military solutions.[4] The January 2012 U.S. Department of Defense *Planning Guidance* established a framework for rethinking the role of land forces to gain more integrative capacity from America's allies and partners. Especially important was a focus on Europe which stated that: "In keeping with this evolving strategic landscape, our posture in Europe must also evolve." The document added that: "Whenever possible, we will develop innovative, low-cost, and small-footprint approaches to achieve our security objectives."[5] This language was a significant shift from the 2010 *Quadrennial Defense Review* (QDR) report, which called for maintaining 400,000 military personnel either forward-stationed or rotationally deployed to "help sustain U.S. capacity for global reach and power protection." The 2010 QDR did call for a "new architecture of cooperation, one that generates opportunities for the U.S. to work together with allies and partners on shared regional and global security opportunities and challenges." It declared that the United States will "continue to develop its defense posture to enhance other states' abilities to solve global security problems."[6] Thus a conceptual approach for rebalancing relations between allies and partners is in place — even if the main driver of the difference between 2010 and 2012 was the economy. However, the expectation that allies might fill in gaps has not been met. This risks producing a hollow alliance with over-ambitious goals and insufficient focus on core security priorities.[7]

The current driver of American thinking on overseas land forces presence is the budget and long-term debt exacerbated by a near doubling of defense spending between 2001 and 2012. The then over $14 trillion debt was identified by former Secretary of State Hillary Clinton and former Chairman of the Joint Chiefs of Staff Admiral Mike Mullen as a national security threat which increased U.S. vulnerabilities. The 2013 automatic spending cuts loomed heavy on the U.S. Armed Forces — imposing decisions that would be better guided by strategic prioritization. By early-2013, the Army indicated it would be cutting up to 30 percent of its operations and maintenance budget, warning that all commands should "slow spending now and plan for the worst."[8] The 2013 automatic spending cuts also included the potential furlough of up to 800,000 defense civilians engaged in critical functions of intelligence, logistics, contracting, and health care.[9] The impact of congressional gridlock put at risk Army readiness accounts by $17-19 billion, according to Army Chief of Staff General Ray Odierno.[10] These cuts were painful, but were also a result of the defense budget having gotten larger than was necessary, given the evolving nature of global security requirements.[11] Cuts would impact readiness if the existing strategy remained in place. However, if alternative strategic options exist that include less reliance on permanent overseas deployments, then readiness need not suffer as much. The question of "ready to do what" remains unanswered. If the mission is scaled back and allies and partners are more capable of providing for their own security, then fewer U.S. forces are needed, and those remaining can be sustained at appropriate readiness levels.

The case for new strategic priorities is supported by U.S. domestic public opinion trends. The 2012 Chicago Council on Foreign Relations survey showed that 71 percent of the American public felt that recent experiences in wars should make the United States more cautious about using military force to deal with rogue states.[12] While only 38 percent want the United States to stay out of world affairs altogether, this was the highest measure of isolationist sentiment since World War II (52 percent of those surveyed between the ages of 18 to 29 agreed with this sentiment). Most Americans—56 percent—believe the United States should prioritize working through the United Nations (UN) even when it means not always getting the preferred outcome. Only 7 percent of the American public disagreed with the "lead from behind" model in the 2011 Libya war. On Afghanistan, only 17 percent supported leaving American combat forces there after 2014, and 54 percent opposed long-term basing. Overall, 68 percent of the American public support cutting defense spending, while only 32 percent believe it should be left unchanged. As to American treaty-based allies, only South Korea receives strong support, 60 percent, for long-term basing. By a split of 50-49 percent, Americans oppose defending Israel if it were to be attacked by a neighbor; by a split of 56-41 percent, Americans oppose defending South Korea if it is attacked; and by a split of 69-28 percent, Americans oppose defending Taiwan against an attack from China. Strong majorities support direct diplomatic talks with Iran and North Korea—67 and 69 percent, respectively.

Global trends, budget realities, and public opinion combine to provide for a climate that has the United States seeking "more" from allies and partners. Missing, however, has been a clear plan to achieve this outcome. Instead, U.S. policy has perpetuated a strategy that, at best, tolerates and, at worst, encourages, free-riding on American military power. The time is right to add strategy and a plan to the emerging trends that are driving American thinking on Landpower. Landpower is the important priority for deployment realignments because American air and naval forces can work in conjunction with local ground forces when needed, while ground forces can be held in reserve and rotational in their training. There are, however, obstacles that must be surmounted if the United States is to rely more on its allies and partners as an entire transatlantic strategic, political, and operational culture must change.

STRUCTURAL OBSTACLES TO BURDENSHARING: THE COSTS OF PRIMACY

During and after the Cold War, America pursued a strategy that sustained primacy among allies and, while demanding more contributions, worked to prevent independent European efforts.[13] Unequal burden sharing was tolerable for the United States in exchange for American say over European security and a benefit to allies who allocated resources toward economic priorities. The forward presence of American Landpower in Germany (and Japan) reassured neighbors as Europe progressed away from World War II images into a peaceful society, while deterring the Soviet Union.[14] This was not, however, envisioned by early Cold War strategic planners as a permanent state of affairs. George Kennan (the architect of "containment") warned during the negotiations that created NATO:

> Instead of the ability to divest ourselves gradually of the basic responsibility for the security of Western Europe, we will get a legal perpetuation of that responsibility. In the long-run, such a legalistic structure must crack up on the rocks of reality; for a divided Europe is not permanently viable, and the political will of the U.S. people is not sufficient to enable us to support Western Europe indefinitely as a military appendage.[15]

Yet, during the Cold War, on average the United States spent about 6.5 percent of its gross domestic product (GDP) on defense, while the European allies spent about 3 percent (lower if one excludes high-spending Greece and Turkey). Today, while the United States has sustained higher percentages of defense spending, the European averages have cascad-

75

ed. As Barry Posen observes, while the United States now spends about 4.6 percent of its GDP on defense, the Europeans are spending collectively 1.6 percent (mainly on salaries and personnel support — a dilemma increasingly also affecting the United States — not hard capabilities that might complement American power in a crisis). Posen writes that:

> With their high per capita GDPs, these allies can afford to devote more money to their militaries, and yet they have no incentive to do so. And while the U.S. government considers draconian cuts in social spending to restore the United States' fiscal health, it continues to subsidize the security of Germany and Japan. This is welfare for the rich.[16]

NATO illustrates how these structural constraints make it difficult to achieve more spending by allies and partners to offset U.S. costs and deliver better capabilities. Even during the dangerous days of the Cold War, domestic pressures rose in the United States about the cost and lack of operational burden sharing among the European allies in NATO.[17] As Senator Mike Mansfield stated in an effort to advance legislation to rebalance NATO:

> The commitment by all Members of the North Atlantic Treaty is based upon the full cooperation of all Treaty partners in contributing materials and men on a fair and equitable basis, but such contributions have not been forthcoming from all the Members ... the present policy of maintaining large contingents of U.S. forces and their dependents ... also contributes further to the fiscal and monetary problems of the U.S.[18]

Rather than rebalance this dynamic after the Cold War, new missions ran apace of the will of the members to provide sufficient capabilities. By taking on both more members and missions without first aligning goals and means, the alliance was challenged with a disconnect among incentives that exacerbated burden sharing imbalances between the United States and its NATO allies.[19] Programs like the Partnership for Peace and eventual membership in NATO provided politically eager new members, but few advances in capabilities. Moreover, once new members joined NATO, their incentives to reform and increase capabilities to be contributors to, and not consumers of, security, declined.[20] NATO was, in fact, on course to becoming politically unmanageable, militarily dysfunctional, and strategically unable to adapt to new security and economic requirements.

Relative to America's and Europe's global position, the European allies and partners have contributed significant levels of troops, for example into Afghanistan where 90 percent of the (up to 40,000) non-U.S. troops serving there in the International Security Assistance Force (ISAF) were European. Europeans also provide a high percentage of UN peacekeeping forces around the world. Still, the ability to assume the burden of leadership by European allies and partners is in steady decline. American officials and NATO secretary generals have called on the allies to invest more in capabilities, and NATO ministers have made repeated commitments to increase defense investments.[21] These goals have persistently fallen short because European national interests were not commensurate with changes in the incentive structure of reliance on American power. Operationally, NATO proved effective in Bosnia in 1995 as a means of peace enforcement following the Dayton Accords. The initial force there consisted of 60,000 troops, half of which were American and half made up of allies and partners.[22] Over time, the United States was able to hand over lead responsibility in Bosnia to forces organized by European allies, so that by 2013, Europe provided 90 percent of all forces for peacekeeping operations (there and in Kosovo). But as additive missions grew more intensive and further afield, the capacity to organize effective coalitions became increasingly difficult, and gaps between American and allied will and capacity widened.

The 1999 Kosovo war exposed major problems with force projection and a disconnect between strategy and allied and partner land forces. According to NATO commander Admiral James O. Ellis, in Kosovo NATO conducted a "war by committee" which negatively affected "every aspect of planning and execution" as it led to incremental war instead of decisive action. This had negative effects on Joint Task Force activation, staff composition, facilities, command and control, logistics and execution, component staffing, and target selection.[23] The United States was unwilling to share information on key strategic assets like F-117s, B2s, and cruise missiles, and the allies could not agree on planning for a ground threat to make air power more effective. This experience led the United States to avoid the alliance in the early years of the Afghanistan war following the terrorist attacks of September 2001. NATO assumed command of Afghan operations in 2005, but land forces became problematic in terms of strategy and tactics. Allied and partner contributions were insufficient, often the wrong kinds of forces, lacked full capacity for army and police training, and were hindered by "caveats" restricting allied deployments and undermining unity of command. Essential combat forces and related supporting material — airlift, strategic intelligence, satellite surveillance, unmanned air vehicles, troop carrying helicopters, attack helicopters, and experienced special operations forces—were primarily American during the war.

In 2011, Libya was a major turning point as the United States sought to "lead from behind"—supporting a NATO intervention, but with allied countries out front. Allies were able to fly (in total) 75 percent of all combat air operations and 100 percent of maritime operations. Yet, only a handful of NATO members provided forces while capable allies and partners, especially Germany, provided no forces for the operation. Among the contributing allies (France and Britain, with support from Belgium, Canada, Denmark, and Norway), NATO could not operate basic airlift, precision-guided weaponry, and sustainable air operations and, like in Kosovo, no ground force was contemplated. American forces were essential to the early phases of the campaign which required attacking Libyan air defenses so allied and partner aircraft could fly unhindered. A month into the Libya campaign, the United States was flying about 25 percent of air activity over Libya—mainly intelligence, jamming, and refueling operations.[24] Britain used almost 20 percent of its cruise missile stockpiles in the first 3 weeks of the war.[25] NATO members could not agree why they were bombing, with official policy being to provide humanitarian relief—but the actual mission was regime change.

This operational imbalance in NATO has reached its apex at the moment America increasingly wishes to hand over the lead to its allies and partners, yet they are concurrently either unwilling or ill-equipped to do so. Just on air transport alone, the U.S.-European ratio within NATO was, by 2011, 285-16 for long-range heavy transport and 632-205 for medium range deployments.[26] The United States provides for 75 percent of total NATO spending—though when considering direct outlays for European security concerns, this figure changes, relative to direct NATO budgets of which the United States pays 25 percent (high for a single ally), with 75 percent of those costs paid by other NATO members collectively. Direct costs of maintaining the troop presence in Europe is relatively low—in the low billions of dollars—and it would likely cost more to relocate U.S. troops out of Europe in the near term than to sustain them.[27] Larger costs are hidden in the inability of allies to operate in multinational and joint force projection contingencies without the United States and its costly defense procurement. Some allies, like Germany, would have to double defense spending to reach NATO's official goal of 2 percent of GDP. With Germany, the challenge is mainly how it spends money as it has 200,000 troops but only about 9,000 available for overseas deployment.[28] Meanwhile, for example, Britain faces major delays in deploying its aircraft carrier fleet and is having continued debate over its Trident nuclear arsenal; Spain finds maintaining its aircraft carrier to be costly; Denmark has eliminated its submarine program; and the Dutch eliminated their tanks.[29]

The dynamic of overpromising NATO's reach while undersupplying allied and partner capacities creates what Barry Posen refers to as a "moral hazard." Allies and partners might erroneously think that the United States will be there to defend them if they get into trouble. Posen notes, for example, regarding the war between Russia and (U.S. partner) Georgia in 2008:

... Georgia acted far too adventurously given its size, proximity to Russia, and distance from any plausible source of military help. . . . This needless war ironically made Russia look tough and the United States unreliable.[30]

Thus in August 2008, the Polish Prime Minister said regarding the general reluctance in NATO to secure Georgia against what Warsaw's politicians saw as Russian neo-imperialist threats: "Poland and the Poles do not want to be in alliances in which assistance comes at some point later—it is no good when assistance comes to dead people."[31]

Europe is capable of providing for its defense and peripheral crisis management. It is a region with two nuclear powers (Britain and France) and has over two million people collectively in uniform. America's European allies spend considerably on defense, collectively second only to the United States in global terms. Moreover, Europeans have fought and spilled blood alongside American troops, especially in Afghanistan. American soldiers repeatedly relate stories of the fighting will of allies and partners. Still, others collectively refer to the NATO acronym for the Afghan force—ISAF—as "I Saw Americans Fight." Overall, only a few allies provide most of that spending—the United Kingdom (UK), France, Germany, Italy, and Spain. While the United States spends 31 percent of its defense budget on investment, the European allies spend 22 percent, which is widening a transatlantic capabilities gap. Much of that European spending is duplicative due to national defense industrial priorities.[32] In 2013, France sent 2,400 ground troops in an intervention into the African country of Mali to combat radical Islamic militias with links to al-Qaeda. The

French force was small, but the remaining total European contribution was just 450 people, for a post-crisis training mission. As Daniel Keohane writes: "Many Europeans send soldiers on peacekeeping missions, but as we saw it in Libya, as we see in Mali, not so many countries are willing to do real shooting, or fighting, or bombing."[33] Some French officials preferred to act as the lead force without the constraints of allies, despite having returned to the NATO military command structure in 2009. As French Colonel Michel Goya said in January 2013: "We have more freedom of action if we do it alone than if we go through NATO procedures. It would be even worse at the EU level. If we do it alone, it's more efficient in military terms."[34]

France is able, at least on paper, to deploy up to 30,000 troops on force projection operations. It, however, could not do the Mali operation alone and had little choice but to turn to Washington for staging, airlift, intelligence, and other logistical operations. Britain also contributed airlift for French troops and equipment, surveillance aircraft, and 400 soldiers in noncombat roles.[35] This absence of European capacity underscored high costs to the United States, even when an ally tried to lead. For example, the C-17 cargo planes, which the United States contributed to move French troops and equipment, cost about $225 million per plane to procure. This costs the United States about $4.5 billion in terms of new planes and existing maintenance of procurements, and about $12,000 per hour to fly. Personnel costs run about $385,000 per service member associated with each plane, which grow higher with training costs for pilots not counting retirement and other associated long-term costs.[36] Since 2008, the United States has developed a multinational heavy airlift operation based in Hungary, the

C-17 Heavy Airlift Wing, which integrates a range of new NATO allies and partners like Sweden and Finland, and operating costs are shared in maintaining three C-17s. This is a small operation, with only 150 personnel required, but depends on American equipment (which has its base in the U.S. Air Mobility Command). Since 2009, this wing has flown more than 500 missions, transported more than 29,000 passengers, and delivered more than 22,000 tons of equipment and supplies—mostly to support operations in Afghanistan.[37] Still, while this is a model of effective multilateral cooperation on airlift, it is small and could not operate without costly American procurement and logistical support.

Gates told a 2011 Brussels meeting that NATO faced a "dim, if not dismal, future" and that:

> there will be a dwindling appetite and patience in the U.S. Congress—and in the American body politic writ large—to expend increasingly precious funds on behalf of nations that are apparently unwilling to devote the necessary resources or make the necessary changes to be serious and capable partners in their own defense.

Gates added that some allies are "apparently willing and eager for American taxpayers to assume the growing security burden left by reductions in European defense budgets."[38] Gates' successor, Leon Panetta, echoed this warning in October 2011, stating that: "We need to use this moment to make the case for the need to invest in this alliance, to ensure it remains relevant to the security challenges of the future."[39] By 2013, a dangerous nexus of shifting priorities converged, summarized by Judy Dempsey: "The United States won't lead in Europe and its neighborhood anymore, and the European powers are not ready to act in concert to take collective responsibility."[40] This perspective was echoed by outgoing Secretary of Defense Leon Panetta, who said in February 2013 that:

> There's no question that in the current budget environment, with deep cuts in European defense spending and the kind of political gridlock that we are seeing in the United States right now with regards to our own budget, [it] is putting at risk our ability to effectively act together. . . . I do fear that the alliance will soon be — if it is not already — stretched too thin.[41]

Nevertheless, mired in the Eurozone crisis and with even greater calls for austerity-driven budget cuts across Europe, little action appeared likely to change the transatlantic dynamic. Thus the columnist George Will asked incoming Secretary of Defense Chuck Hagel in January 2013 to explain of NATO:

> What is its purpose now? Given that U.S. military spending is three times larger than the combined spending of NATO's other 27 members, is it not obvious that those nations feel no threat? . . . Might fewer than 54,000 U.S. forces in Germany suffice to defend that country, or Western Europe, from whatever threat they are there to deter?[42]

THE CASE FOR REBALANCING NATO

The case for rebalancing NATO via major cuts in America's land forces presence in Europe is strong. This is especially true because the operating assumption that American troop cuts will lead to more spending from the allies and partners in Europe is not viable. Writing in 2012, Dr. John Deni notes significant U.S. troop withdrawals:

From a high point of over a quarter-million Solders in Europe at the height of the Cold War, the U.S. Army has drawn down to roughly 42,000 Soldiers today. . . . Plans announced in early 2012 call for further cuts between now and 2014, when two of the four remaining U.S. brigade combat teams in Europe will activate, bringing the total down to roughly 29,000 Soldiers by 2014.[43]

Yet, these withdrawals have not led to any notable increases in European contributions.

The European allies do not see threats that require increasing defense spending—even among new allies to the East who have closer memories of historical Russian aggression. NATO Europe overall defense spending fell by 3.7 percent a year between 2008 and 2010, by 2.6 percent in 2011, and by 1.54 percent in 2012.[44]. The allies in Europe are amenable to peripheral operations—like Libya—if assisted by the United States. Moreover, the gap in defense spending is also exacerbated by the dramatic increases in U.S. spending since 2001. The fundamental problem is structural, in that allies and partners in Europe are not incentivized to better pool resources to act independently from the United States.

Until the United States announces a plan for rebalancing NATO, the relative incentives for allies to better coordinate resources will remain unchanged. Almost a year after pronouncements of new capabilities cooperation at the May 2012 NATO Summit in Chicago, a report from the German Foreign Ministry indicated that, within NATO: "It has not been possible to achieve any consensus in core areas."[45] Part of the problem relates to concerns about Germany itself, which is increasingly seen by other allies as unreliable for undertaking force projection missions in a crisis. At the same time, what is described crucially as a "culture of military restraint" in Germany might also be seen as "mission accomplished" in terms of the original missions of NATO—the Russians are out, the Germans are down, so why then, are the Americans kept "in"? Ultimately, as German defense analyst Rainer Arnold puts it: "Everyone is doing his own thing without taking the others into account."[46] While Russia remains a concern to some NATO allies, its mobilization timelines are significantly distant for any serious conventional threat requiring Article 5 commitments in NATO. Russia could seek to exert influence among allies that might affect strategic alignments—but that is already happening, for example, with gas flows and energy dependence, and has little to do with American troop deployments in Europe. This is a strategic vulnerability, but one that reinforces the point that many emerging security challenges are not amenable to forward deployed Landpower and thus require new operational frameworks.

By 2013, total U.S. forces assigned to Europe included 80,000 military personnel in 28 main operating bases—including 35,000 Soldiers, 25,000 Airmen and women, 10,000 Sailors and Marines, with about 64,000 assigned to U.S. European Command (EUCOM) operations. These are supported by an additional 16,000 civilians and contractors. Total costs of housing and operational support between 2006 and 2009 was $17 billion.[47] The United States is engaged in an ongoing drawdown of land forces in Europe.[48] By 2014, the 170th Brigade Combat Team in Baumholder, Germany, and the 172nd Brigade Combat Team based in Grafenwoehr, Germany, will be inactivated. The Army's V Corps Headquarters, based in Heidelberg,

Germany, will not return to Europe after their deployment in Afghanistan ends. Meanwhile, the Air Force A-10 squadron based in Spangdahalem Air Base in Germany and the 603rd Air Control squadron at Aviano Air Base in Italy will return to the United States. These closures or redeployments will save an estimated $2 billion over 10 years. Consolidation of other bases will allow for savings for support infrastructure of an additional $112 million.[49] Additional realignments were announced in February 2013 with members of the Europe-based 173rd Brigade Combat Team being realigned out of Germany into Italy, including the 173rd's Special Troops Battalion and its Support Battalion. These moves allow the United States to close bases in Bamberg and Schweinfurt, Germany.[50] The United States will maintain logistical and equipment support in Europe for a rotational brigade combat team committed to the NATO Response Force.

According to EUCOM, the U.S. Department of Defense (DoD) is engaged in a "theater-wide capacity analysis as part of a comprehensive consolidation of its overseas infrastructure in light of these force posture changes. . . . The result could be further infrastructure adjustments."[51] According to Lieutenant General Mark Hertling, this will limit American ability to train with allies in that "we are going to have to reduce our partnerships."[52] This assumption is valid if one assumes that America needs large numbers of forces interacting with allies and partners. It is not the case, however, if America's goal is to play a small advisory role in helping allies and partners to better coordinate on their own. By 2013, American military commanders in Europe felt that a total of 30,000 U.S. land forces, enhanced via rotations and new commitments to NATO's Response Force, would be adequate for sustaining the existing mission. However, the mission itself has not been reviewed. Thus, there is no inherent logic that said the proper number was 30,000, 15,000, 3-5,000 or even zero.

Meanwhile, Congress is signaling growing political support for deeper cuts in U.S. land forces presence in Europe. In March 2013, Senator Bob Corker (ranking Republican on the Senate Foreign Relations Committee) said: "[O]ur NATO allies are not carrying their weight, forcing American service members and taxpayers to bear the heaviest burden in NATO-led missions."[53] While it did not survive in the U.S. Senate, the House of Representatives passed (226-196) a resolution in December 2012 calling for the removal of all permanent American troops from Europe. The House language noted:

> Congress finds that, because defense spending among European NATO countries fell 12 percent since 2008, from $314 billion to $275 billion, so that currently only four out of the 28 NATO allies of the United States are spending the widely agreed-to standard of 2 percent of their GDP on defense, the United States must look to more wisely allocate scarce resources to provide for the national defense. [54]

The House recommended that rotational Army deployments would be:

> sufficient to permit the United States to satisfy the commitments undertaken by the United States pursuant to Article 5 of the North Atlantic Treaty . . . (and) address the current security environment in Europe and contribute to peace and stability in Europe.[55]

Even rotational deployments might prove difficult, with just one combat battalion regularly rotating through Europe (for NATO's response force) on a regular basis, as the Pentagon Spokesman George Little said in February 2013 that we are "talking about the prospect of not being able to engage in rotational deployments in Europe" due to budget cuts.[56] Thus there is momentum for hosting exercises with allies and partners in the United States, rather than Europe. Annually, the United States and its European allies and partners carry out dozens of multinational training exercises involving 42 countries and 50,000 U.S., allied, and partner forces in Europe. This helps allies and partners better work alongside American forces, for example, in Afghanistan. However, there is no reason that capable allies cannot pool funding to support the costs of holding exercises in the United States. In fact, by realigning the exercise rotations by allies and partners to the United States, it can better prepare allies for mobilization and force projection outside the European area while gaining interoperability exposure to American capabilities. Additionally, the allies and partners in NATO have gained impressive operational experience in Afghanistan—from which they can now play a major role in training future generations of European forces.

In the last two major wars America has fought, Afghanistan and Iraq, EUCOM's primary role has been as a support mechanism for mobilizations managed by U.S. Central Command (CENTCOM), even for a NATO labeled coalition, which suggests it can be further realigned in a new command structure reform. Currently, EUCOM consists of 64,000 joint forces deployed in the European area located across 21 major bases. EUCOM has as its core mission to ensure a strong NATO alliance, preserve recently developed allied and partner capability and interoperability, and to maintain regional stability and security. Strategically, the presence of EUCOM as a forward deployed regional command perpetuates the structural dependence of allies and partners on the United States for power projection, decreases incentives for allied and partner defense investment and coordination, and perpetuates Europe's dependency on the United States for regional stability and security. Many activities highlighted by EUCOM in its annual report to Congress do not require a heavy permanent presence of American troops to achieve (such as with exercises involving joint command operations for cyber defense). Other elements do require the showing of presence, such as rotational naval exercises in the Baltic Sea and Black Sea conducted by U.S. Naval Forces Europe and including the U.S. Marine Corps Black Sea Rotational Force (which is based in the United States). Thus, elements of EUCOM, such as the Air Command at Ramstein, Germany; the Special Operations headquarters in Stuttgart, Germany; and the U.S. Sixth Fleet based in Naples, Italy, remain important. Unclear in this mix, however, is why the command headquarters is required to remain forward deployed and could not, instead be reduced in size and relocated to the United States. Key command elements, like the Joint Multinational Training Command (JMTC) can assume significant responsibility for engaging with allies and partners to put them in the lead role for future European area security operations.

EUCOM's existing posture is based on forces, footprints, and relationships. Yet the current number of American forces and the size of the large U.S. footprint perpetuate inefficient operational burden sharing relationships that do not benefit the United States. The case for relocating this forward command, perhaps integrating it into the existing NATO strategic command (Allied Command Transformation) in Norfolk, Virginia, is strong. Meanwhile, Allied Command Operations, at Supreme Headquarters Allied Powers Europe in Belgium, could be gradually handed over to European NATO allies for lead responsibility on an agreed timeline, to include a European Supreme Allied Commander, Europe (SACEUR).[57]

The European continent continues to have a geographic role supporting Persian Gulf contingencies via the NATO ballistic missile defense shield. Permanent basing to support this system can become the most visible U.S. commitment to Article 5 NATO planning in the existing threat environment. The command architectures for maritime missile defense elements would remain with the overall command being deployed at Ramstein, Germany. The NATO missile defense plan adapts multiple phases of deployment building on capable and tested theater-based systems via the *Aegis* model in southeastern Europe. These systems require enabling, operational, and command-based American troop deployments, supported by the stationing of four *Aegis* destroyers in Spain and radar facilities in Turkey. This will not, however, require large personnel numbers—just 500 planned for the command base in Ramstein, Germany. Ramstein, meanwhile, remains an important air force operations hub for global communications and operations and for medical facilities, while also providing a symbolic commitment to collective defense.

Europe is not as geographically crucial for supporting conventional Persian Gulf contingencies today as in previous decades. The United States, via CENTCOM, sustains a network of command headquarters, pre-positioning of troops and equipment, and exercising of significant deployment capacity. CENTCOM does require logistical access to European bases, airlift, and refueling of heavy transport coming from the United States. However, the argument for a large presence of American troops available to deploy out of Europe is not as salient as it was in the 1990s. In the first Persian Gulf War (1990-91), logistical necessity required drawing American land forces heavily out of Europe. This is no longer the case, given existing Gulf deployments and the ability to negotiate ad-hoc transit rights via key European countries. Indeed, non-NATO country Ireland (via Shannon Airport) became a critical transport hub through which hundreds of thousands of U.S. forces transited.[58] The newly created Africa Command, based in Stuttgart, Germany, showed that during the 2012 Benghazi crisis in Libya, response times out of Europe were insufficient for emergency deployments and that, at least for crisis deployments, more theater-oriented basing was likely needed. As Army General David M. Rodriguez asserts: "The recent crisis in North Africa demonstrates the volatility of the African security environment," adding that the Africa Command needs drones, surveillance aircraft, and satellite imagery, and the command currently gets only half of its stated needs for North Africa and only 7 percent of total requirements for the continent.[59] Globally, the increased requirements to support the declared "pivot" toward Asia require additional offsetting savings and equipment reallocations.

In the Persian Gulf area of operations, the United States maintains a significant footprint which, in a crisis, can be reinforced from the United States. The 13,000 American troops now based in Kuwait reduce the geographical value that land forces in Europe have played in past Gulf contingencies. These new circumstances bolster the case for cutting land forces allocated to EUCOM to liberate funds to support reassurance efforts among allies and partners in the Persian Gulf (with 13,000 troops already planned for regular stationing in Kuwait). Redeploying too many resources to build up Persian Gulf contingencies can have the unintended effect of exacerbating tensions with Iran and undermining diplomatic engagement, thus having over-the-horizon deployment capacity is important. Too much American presence can make allies and partners in the Persian Gulf nervous. For example, among the 20 states from the region that participated in an early 2013 headquarters and live air, sea, and land drill for interdiction of vessels with illicit weapons on the high seas, most refused to officially confirm their involvement.[60] In February 2013, the DoD announced it would reduce from two to one the aircraft carrier strike groups that patrol the region to save money — about $10 billion a year. According to Chairman of the Joint Chiefs of Staff General Martin Dempsey, "This is the first adjustment of what will be, I think, a series of adjustments across the services as we try to preserve our readiness for as long as possible."[61] Existing Persian Gulf capacity is sufficient for mobilization of U.S. troops into the region. Rather than needing Europe for relocating troops, the case is strong for reallocating resources and seeing Europe more in the context of a logistical hub for transportation from the United States as needed and as a fallback location should basing options in the Persian Gulf change.

Repeated warnings to European allies and partners to do more on capabilities go unheard because the European allies lack incentives to follow suit. They do not feel threatened, they correctly conclude that their major security challenges are economic, and they are comfortable knowing that, in a crisis, the United States can be called on for enabling forces. As Kori Schake argues: "That Europeans don't have these 'enablers' in sufficient supply is their fault. They choose to spend their money differently, predictably reducing military prowess and increasing the risk of failure." Schake argues that the Mali crisis, where Washington took time deciding whether to support France with transport and other capabilities, was not the right moment to make this change.

> The Obama Doctrine depends critically on others stepping forward and undertaking the work we are stepping back from. There will be fewer allies willing to do that if we continue to be stingy with our help and generous with our criticism.[62]

The United States has nonetheless failed to adjust to this basic dynamic of national interests and political economy so as to avoid continued European dependency on the United States for the conduct of military operations. NATO officials have not helped advance this understanding by failing to see the economic crisis as the primary security problem in Europe. For example, in January 2013, NATO Secretary General Anders Fogh Rasmussen inverted the nature of security problems, saying:

> Of course, governments must reduce deficits and borrowing. . . . You can't be safe if you're broke. But . . . we have to invest to keep our societies safe. Because security threats won't go away while we focus on fixing our economies.[63]

Similarly, in a February 2012 testimony before Congress, (reinforced in March 2013) Supreme Allied Commander (and EUCOM commander) Admiral James Stavridis said that the most important reason to keep U.S. troops in Europe is the economic basis of the transatlantic relationship, noting that the "European economy is still about 25 percent of the world's GDP about the same size as that of the United States."[64] In fact, the security threat that most requires fixing is the economy. Unnecessary and duplicative spending on military power in Europe during a major economic crisis is part of the problem, not the solution. One might argue that more European defense spending could create more jobs and adjust for the negative impact of austerity, but this is not an argument that will sell among European publics and political leaders. Thus, aligning goals toward pooling existing resources and long-term defense planning is both incentivized by the Eurozone crisis and also the most realistic long-term policy option.

GEOSPACIAL OPPORTUNITIES FOR SHAPING LAND FORCES COOPERATION

The United States has a historic opportunity to embark on new and vigorous leadership in the transatlantic relationship that can help to reverse NATO's decline and make it viable for the 21st century by creating new incentives to get better capacity among allies and partners. Further American land forces reductions are needed, should have a clearly stated strategic premise, and happen on an agreed timeline. Meanwhile, other elements of the U.S.-European relationship — especially trade — should take a new priority. If, in a time of lasting peace and no over-the-horizon conventional threats, America cannot hand over lead responsibility to allies and partners in Europe, then where in the world can it? There are serious challenges associated with such a shift. In particular, how would the existing NATO command structure be realigned to reflect a European-forward NATO? Would the United States hold a veto authority over European-only style operations — or would a new consensus rule be needed? Would the withdrawal of nearly all U.S. land forces from Europe raise the costs of ad-hoc transit routes to other regions of the world should their land and airspace in Europe be needed? Would a withdrawal of U.S. leadership from non-Article 5 operations lead to a simultaneous withdrawal for Europeans, concluding that if the United States will not do it, they too will not? Would Article 5 have continued credibility at a moment the allies in NATO are not ready or, rather than incentivize integration, reinforce more nationalization in defense capabilities? These are significant questions, but none is insurmountable with effective American leadership that works to make NATO more durable as a basis for allies and partners to assume lead roles. American planners cannot know with certainty that a new approach to realignment within NATO will produce optimal outcomes. They can, however, know for certain that the decades-old existing approach has not produced such outcomes. Some places, such as Kosovo, show us what is possible. Today the United Staates maintains just 10 percent of total NATO mission forces there (Kosovo Forces [KFOR]) — a relative percentage goal that could be a target for all non-Article 5 contingencies involving U.S. troops.

NATO has an enduring function in advancing America's security interests. America should thus play an appropriate role in it. NATO's institutional architectures are important for planning and enhancing logistics and interoperability goals for peace operations and, if necessary, coalition warfare. Today there are over 41 nonallied NATO partners from all over the world. In fact, between capable allies and partners, upwards of 68 nations, come together to study NATO standards, tactics, techniques and procedures, doctrine, and operational concepts.[65] This will be especially true as allies and partners return from Afghanistan with advanced experience in headquarters coordination, staffing, and operational doctrine drawing on, and feeding back into, NATO. NATO, however, does not, by necessity, need current levels of American land forces to sustain and grow itself as a global hub for military planning and information sharing. Moreover, the European nations have both current and latent capability to integrate and coordinate resources effectively if their interests are incentivized to do so.

There is virtually no foreseeable probability of a dramatic renationalization of European defense policies, given deep multilateral military cooperation in NATO and economic integration in the European Union (EU). Britain and France have developed joint operational concepts as have France and Germany, and Germany and Poland for military cooperation — among just a few major examples. Poland has gained confidence in its dealings with Russia since consolidating its position in Central Europe via NATO membership.[66] Moreover, a new view toward Germany is prevailing, according to Foreign Minister Radislaw Sikorski who in November 2011 called Germany Europe's "indispensable nation" and declared that:

> I demand of Germany that, for your sake and ours, you
> help the Eurozone survive and prosper. You know full

well that nobody else can do it. I will probably be the first Polish foreign minister in history to say so, but here it is: I fear German power less than I am beginning to fear German inactivity.[67]

Meanwhile, Poland and France have increased their engagement, sparked by a realization in Warsaw that the United States is shifting out of Europe, and that it must push the EU to do a better job of filling the gap.[68] Given the structural depths of the Eurozone crisis, the United States should not want Europe to spend more on defense.[69] The challenge is thus how to get Europe to spend in ways that complement American security interests. But, overall, America can enjoy the outcome of a successful grand strategy — a Europe that is united, whole, and free, and where traditional security dilemmas are alleviated.

The ongoing European economic crisis is pushing the United States and its European allies to think hard about how to pool existing military resources.[70] Following yet another spending appeal from a NATO secretary general in early 2013, Danish Defense Minister Nick Haekkerup was asked if there was any commitment to increase defense investments once the economy improves. He replied, "No, there isn't. . . ."[71] Small states are making major cuts, for example, through 2015, Lithuania cut defense spending by 36 percent from 2010. The average medium-sized NATO countries will cut defense spending by 10-15 percent, and the larger allies will cut defense spending by about 8 percent.[72] However, as James Stacey notes:

> [T]he shared fiscal austerity has set into motion a host of European efforts to pool their defense capabilities — what the Europeans call pooling and sharing and what NATO refers to as smart defense, or more specifically getting more with less.[73]

Some allies are cutting entire systems; the Dutch are cutting their tank force and transferring the savings to contribute to NATO's new missile defense system.[74] Overall, the allies are cutting expenditures and will be for some time, but this also means that now is an opportune moment for them to realize the national interest in defense consolidation to achieve common security objectives. Meanwhile, allies like France which have sought leadership in Europe should be encouraged—even if it means increased reliance on European models, rather than American, of equipment acquisition. It is a good development, for example, that France has plans for the purchase of A400M transport planes being built by Airbus with the first three of 50 scheduled to arrive in 2013.[75]

Ultimately, large European countries pooling substantial capabilities are what will be necessary for Europe to take on major missions like a Libya-style air campaign and a Balkans-style peace support operation. Some of this is happening when, for example, in 2010 Britain and France announced they will integrate their military capabilities bilaterally and at a level of depth that was never achieved during the Cold War. This includes creating a joint expeditionary force, planned shared use of aircraft carriers (which has proven difficult due to interoperability differences with landing craft), and combined efforts on nuclear weapons safety and effectiveness including unprecedented information sharing on nuclear programs. This bilateral arrangement goes into considerable detail on sharing programs on parts, maintenance, and training for crews of military transport aircraft, independent of reliance on those of the United States. They also planned cooperation on drone planes and a range of technologies for nuclear submarines and military satellites.[76] In announcing the agreement with France, British Prime Minister David Cameron said that this would save "millions of pounds" as part of a larger dynamic of cutting Britain's defense spending. He added: "It's about defending our national interest. It is about practical, hard-headed cooperation between two sovereign countries." Cameron added that this kind of arrangement should be welcome in Washington because: "They'd like us to have the biggest bang for our buck that we possibly can."[77]

NATO "smart defense" initiatives only number about 30 to date, and most are American-led, not allied incentivized. Much larger concepts that bring in large country European forces integrating the smart defense with the EU's "pooling" concept building around large national contributions, such as British and French cooperation growing to include Germany and Poland, could be a major building block.[78] A symbolic movement in this direction came in 2012 when, in drafting a new French White Paper on defense planning (which noted the need for more effort in Europe given the shift of American priorities toward Asia), Paris included in the drafting commission the British ambassador to France and chair of the Munich Security Conference and former German ambassador to the United States Wolfgang Ischinger.[79] Still, bridging the commitment to sovereignty in defense procurement and national military infrastructures will be difficult, as America was the glue that held the alliance together for decades. While the EU has developed battlegroups for crisis deployment, they are small elements and demonstrate (as does the NATO Response Force) the difficulty of relying on integrated multinational forces that are too small. If one element drops out, the entire force structure can collapse, creating major operational inefficiencies. The EU has also failed in its ambition to create a 60,000 man strong response force. Thus, large-end European-based efforts are necessary to assume responsibility for European allies and partners' share of rebalancing the transatlantic relationship. As highly respected NATO historian Lawrence Kaplan puts it: "If Germany could be induced to the budding Anglo-French military collaboration (assuming it is not ephemeral), Europe's role could be more credible."[80]

In November 2012, British Defense Minister Philip Hammond reviewed the experience of Libya, stating that it had "shone a bright light on relative military and political capabilities in terms of who 'could but wouldn't' and who 'would but couldn't'." He added that:

> The bottom line is that Europe, as a whole, needs to do more, at a time when the reality is that, across the continent, aggregate defense expenditure is certain to fall in the short term and, at best, recover slowly in the medium term. . . . So the challenge is stark: if we can't spend more, we must do things differently — maximizing the capability we can collectively squeeze out of the resources we have, increasing inter-operability, closing capability gaps through joint working and greater specialization.[81]

Or, as German defense analyst Constanze Stellzenmuelle puts it: "Nobody needs 27 air forces and 27 navies. . . .We're all broke."[82] Britain is signaling confidence in the strategic environment by announcing in March 2013 that in the next 6 years, it will have withdrawn all of its troops permanently stationed in Germany. According to Philip Hammond:

The return of the British Army from Germany marks the end of an era, and I want to put on record the huge debt of gratitude we owe to the German Government and the German people for the support, both moral and material, they have shown our Armed Forces over more than 6 decades.[83]

There is thus little logic that America should keep land forces in Germany if the British are not. As heavy American armor units with little operational utility are leaving Europe, it could be useful for the United States to keep one infantry and armored cavalry combat brigade in Germany mainly as a symbolic gesture. However, if the collective defense threat-level is low enough for just one, it is hard to justify.

In April 2013, Europe became American "tank free" for the first time since World War II as its final heavy armor capabilities were withdrawn, a strong indicator that American military planners do not see conventional Article 5 threats to the NATO area even remotely over the horizon. Moreover, if it is the case that land forces remain a visable and important signal of national or multinational commitments, even without the United States, the European allies collectively maintain large numbers of tanks. Land forces have been, and remain, important in the European operational context for non-Article 5 operations. Every major war fought through NATO—from Bosnia to Libya—was decided by facts on the ground. But, in each of these situations, it also was not **American land forces** that were decisive. Rather, it was a combination of American and allied air power and partner forces in support of ground troops that determined outcomes. From the Croat-Muslim alliance in Bosnia to the Kosovo Liberation Army in Kosovo to anti-Qaddafi forces rallying in Libya, land forces remained critical. But they did not need to be Americans.

RECOMMENDATIONS

In March 2013, the DoD announced it was launching a new strategy review to "examine the choices that underlie the Department of Defense's strategy, force posture, investments, and institutional management—including all past assumptions, systems, and practices."[84] In keeping with this examination a new set of American-led policy initiatives can offer a new strategic vision for a realigned transatlantic relationship:

- *Limit America's primary role in NATO to Article 5, collective defense missions.* This means, given the lack of conventional military threats to Europe, placing America's land forces contributions in strategic reserve, hedging against unforeseen changes in the existing security environment or shocks to the international system which require mobilization through NATO. In the contemporary threat environment, this means removing nearly all permanently based U.S. Soldiers in Europe, with the exception of those needed for European ballistic missile defense and limited command headquarters staff contributions and training. America could, as needed, contribute to European-led non-Article 5 operations, as happened in Libya and Mali, but limited to an outcome similar to contemporary Kosovo where America's operational engagement is no more than 10 percent of the total, and the goal is eventually zero.

- *Achieve NATO consensus that the European allies, acting through NATO, would develop an integrated capacity to conduct a Balkans-style peace support operation and a Libya style war without the*

United States. Such an outcome would require a 3-5 year period of planning and development between the United States and its allies. The stated goal would be that primary responsibility for security provision around Europe will be that of the European allies. This also means ceding more say to lead allies on the strategic outcomes of crisis management. This would not mean that in cases where high American interests are at stake, the United States would not participate. Moreover, it would also not signal to the allies that they are completely on their own. Via a clear timeline and a managed process that, as in Mali, signals that America will be available if backstopping is required, the ties that bind the United States and its allies can be sustained but within a new European-led operational context.

- *Move EUCOM to the United States and Make a European SACEUR for non-Article 5 Missions.* The United States should remain in the NATO integrated military command and continue its presence in NATO military committees and planning processes. But there is little logic to suggest the expense of keeping EUCOM via the headquarters presence in Germany, especially when two wars in the last decade were run out of CENTCOM in Florida aided by its forward presence for command and control. The basing of the command of NATO's missile defense shield alongside America's European air command in Ramstein, Germany, and the 6th Fleet headquarters in Naples, Italy, can sustain the on-the-ground presence of a major operational theater command in Europe, and at lower levels should Europeans better coordinate their capabilities. Meanwhile, there is no reason that the SACEUR should not be a European commander when assigned to non-Article 5 operations, while an American commander would retain authority for Article 5 contingency planning, exercising, and operations.

- *Sustain the "Smart Defense" initiative by prioritizing European defense industrial foundations.* The NATO plans to continue to develop "Smart Defense" as pooling capabilities can and should drive operational concepts both for European-led operations and, where possible and appropriate, prioritize European-based acquisition projects and U.S.-European Union (European Defense Agency) joint projects. Meanwhile, allies will need to move away from heavy personnel costs and more mobile forces operating in multilateral environments. "Smart Defense" initiatives will need to incorporate large-end force integration concepts for sustainable operations absent the United States.

- *Plan regular rotation of allied and partner training exercises in the United States and Europe.* Regular command, staff and live action training can occur in American facilities while Americans rotate training through Europe on a periodic schedule. NATO's core institutional attributes, in particular its headquarters in Brussels and the military headquarters in Mons, Belgium, can be re-envisioned for operational activities among allies and partners as a hub for European and global information-sharing and planning funded and operated by European NATO members and partners. Make the combat brigade allocated to the NATO response force a reserve allocation, so that the response force is capable of standing up on its own without U.S. involvement. Meanwhile, low-staffing but high impact operational activities such as information sharing over emerging threats like energy security and cyber security are important for sustaining transatlantic security cooperation without requiring a heavy and costly U.S. land presence.

- *Pivot back to Europe — via a U.S.-EU free trade agreement.* A new free trade agreement will deepen the ties that bind America and Europe on issues that matter most — economic stability and growth. By renewing the economic aspects of the transatlantic relationship, the United States and Europe will show that a realigned NATO does not mean reduction in the fundamentals of the mutual ties that bind the Atlantic community of nations. More broadly, the political foundations of the transatlantic relations — a community of democratic values linked across the Atlantic — would be reinforced, while less pressure is put on the military aspect of the broader strategic relationship.

This is a unique opportunity for President Barack Obama and the European leaders to embark on a historic renewal of the transatlantic relationship by completing a founding vision of NATO — a Europe that is capable of assuming responsibility for its own security.

CONCLUSION

A frequent argument against a near complete withdrawal of American permanent land forces from Europe is that, if the American footprint is not there, the successes in Europe since World War II may unravel. In reality, there is more than sufficient capacity and time to manage such geostrategic fluctuations, as improbable as they are. In fact, this argument ignores these very successes in American strategic positioning toward Europe since 1945. It ignores the deep integration of the European economies, and in particular their capacity if properly incentivized, to pool capabilities that can act alone or complement American power in the world. The case for the status quo ignores the fact that at the most dangerous moment for NATO, the earliest years of the Cold War when hundreds of thousands of Soviet troops remained perched in Eastern Europe and could have advanced into the West, they were deterred. They were deterred, not by land forces from 1949-50, but deterred by the political commitment America made to European security. That commitment, at its most dangerous moment, had no forward deployed land forces, it had no integrated military plans, it had no NATO headquarters, and no secretary general. It was, as the *Porgy and Bess* song played at the NATO treaty signing ceremony in 1949 said, "Plenty of Nothin." It is time for America to make clear to its European friends that it is their moment to lead, and the United States will help them. If there is any place in the world that America can hand over lead responsibility to allies and partners for security management, it is in Europe, and the time is now.

ENDNOTES - CHAPTER 3

1. See Office of the Deputy Undersecretary of Defense, "Department of Defense Base Structure Report: Fiscal Year 2011 Baseline," Washington, DC: U.S. Department of Defense (DoD), 2010.

2. Thom Shanker, "Warning Against Wars Like Iraq and Afghanistan," *New York Times*, February 25, 2011.

3. For an overview of European force reductions and planned reductions to date, see Andrew Feickert, "Army Drawdown and Restructuring: Background and Issues for Congress," Congressional Research Service, 7-5700, Washington, DC: Congressional Research Service, March 5, 2013. Also see Michelle Tan, "Leaving Europe Behind," *Army Times*, April 1, 2013.

4. For further detail, see Sean Kay, *Global Security in the Twenty-first Century: The Quest for Power and the Search for Peace*, 2nd Ed., Lanham, MD: Rowman and Littlefield, 2011.

5. U.S. Department of Defense, "Sustaining U.S. Global Leadership: Priorities for 21st Century Defense," Washington, DC: DoD, 2012, p. 3, available from *www.defense.gov/news/defense_strategic_guidance.pdf*.

6. *Ibid.*

7. See Hans Binnendijk, "A Leaner NATO Needs a Tighter Focus," *New York Times*, February 3, 2012. Advocates of a sustained land forces presence in Europe note that NATO had already cut personnel at its headquarters in Europe by 67 percent in the last decade, and by over 80 percent since the end of the Cold War.

8. Lance M. Bacon, "Belt-tightening Orders," *Army Times*, January 28, 2013.

9. *Ibid.*

10. Sydney J. Freedberg, Jr., "Odierno: Army Faces $17B Readiness Cuts; CH-47 MYP At Risk," *AOL Defense*, January 24, 2013.

11. See, for example, Admiral Gary Roughead, U.S. Navy (Ret.) and Kori Schake, "National Defense in a Time of Change," Washington, DC: The Brookings Institution, February 2013.

12. Survey data references are from the 2012 Chicago Council Survey, available at *www.thechicagocouncil.org/files/Surveys/2012/files/Studies_Publications/POS/Survey2012/2012.aspx*.

13. See Sean Kay, *NATO and the Future of European Security*, Lanham, MD: Rowman and Littlefield, 1998.

14. For a detailed argument on the benefits of American primacy, see Stephen G. Brooks and William C. Wohlforth, *World Out of Balance: International Relations and the Challenge of American Primacy*, Princeton, NJ: Princeton University Press, 2008.

15. "Memorandum of the Director of the Policy Planning Staff, November 29, 1948," *Foreign Relations of the United States*, 1948, pp. 283-289.

16. Barry Posen, "Pull Back: The Case for a Less Activist Foreign Policy," *Foreign Affairs*, Vol. 92, No. 1, January/February 2013, p. 121. For an alternative argument, see Stephen G. Brooks, G. John Ikenberry, and William C. Wolforth, "Don't Come Home, America," *International Security*, Vol. 37, No. 3, Winter 2012/13, pp. 7-51. The authors warn that a premature departure from Europe by the United States might lead to (p.35):

> A Europe that is incapable of securing itself from various threats that could be destabilizing within the region and beyond (e.g., a regional conflict akin to the 1990s Balkan wars), lacks capacity for global security missions in which the U.S. leaders might want European participation, and is vulnerable to the influence of outside rising powers.

17. See Stanley R. Sloan, *Permanent Alliance: The Transatlantic Bargain from Truman to Obama*, New York: Bloomsbury Academic, 2010.

18. United States Senate, "United States Troops in Europe: Hearings Before the Combined Subcommittee of Foreign Relations and Arms Services Committee on the Subject of United States Troops in Europe," 90th Cong., 1st Sess., Washington, DC: U.S. Senate, April 26 and May 3, 1967.

19. Joseph Lepgold, "NATO's Collective Action Problem," *International Security*, Vol. 13, No. 1, Summer 1998, p. 79.

20. See Sean Kay, "What Went Wrong with NATO?" *Cambridge Review of International Affairs*, Vol. 18, No. 1, April 2005, pp. 69-83.

21. See, for example, "Summit Declaration on Defense Capabilities: Towards NATO Forces 2020," NATO, Chicago Summit, May 2012, available from *www.nato.int/cps/en/natolive/official_texts_87594.htm?mode=pressrelease*. This declaration was notable for the amount of attention and encouragement that NATO gave to advanced development of European Union capabilities, something that the United States had previously endorsed only so long as there was no duplication or undermining of NATO.

22. See Kay, *NATO and the Future*.

23. Admiral James O. Ellis, U.S. Navy, "A View from the Top," briefings slides provided to the author by U.S. Department of Defense, Fall 1999.

24. Karen De Young and Greg Jaffe, "NATO Runs Short on Some Munitions in Libya," *Washington Post*, April 15, 2011.

25. Thomas Harding, "Libya: Navy Running Short of Tomahawk Missiles," *The Telegraph*, March 23, 2011.

26. International Institute of Strategic Studies, *The Military Balance: 2011*, London, UK: Routledge, 2011, pp. 38-39.

27. Clara Marina O'Donnell, ed., *The Implications of Military Spending Cuts for NATO's Largest Members*, Washington, DC: The Brookings Institution, July 2012.

28. Paul Ames, "Europe's Army," *Global Post*, January 27, 2013.

29. Tomas Valasek, "NATO Ponders Austerity and U.S. 'Pivot'," International Institute for Strategic Studies, *The Military Balance: 2013*, London: Routledge, 2013, p. 95, available from *centreforeuropeanreform.blogspot.com/2012/05/nato-ponders-austerity-and-us-pivot.html*. In 2012, Spain cut its peacekeeping presence in Lebanon by 50 percent, saw increased discussion of an accelerated withdrawal from Afghanistan, and announced a delay in accepting delivery of 15 *Typhoon* aircraft initially contracted to be delivered between 2012 and 2013. Delays in purchase of other systems, including AM400M transport aircraft, were being considered.

30. Posen, p. 122.

31. Thomas Shanker and Nicholas Kulish, "Russia Lashes Out on Missile Deal," *New York Times*, August 15, 2008.

32. Judy Dempsey, "How Much Are Americans Willing to Spend to Defend Europe?" *International Herald Tribune*, January 7, 2013.

33. Ames.

34. Andrew Rettman, "French Colonel: France Better Off Alone in Mali," *EUObserver.com*, January 13, 2013.

35. Peter Dominiczak, "More than 300 British Troops Will Be Sent to Africa," *The Telegraph*, January 29, 2013.

36. This data is compiled by Phillip Carter, "The French Connection," *Foreign Policy.com*, January 23, 2013.

37. Major Rich Kromurek, "Airlift Airmen Build Multinational Partnerships," *Military.com*, November 2, 2012.

38. Thom Shanker, "Defense Secretary Warns NATO of 'Dim Future'," *New York Times*, June 10, 2011.

39. Stephen Erlanger, "Panetta Urges Europe to Spend More on NATO or Risk a Hollowed Out Alliance," *New York Times*, October 5, 2011.

40. Judy Dempsey, "Mali and Europe's Hard Power," January 25, 2013, available from *carnegieeurope.eu/strategiceurope*.

41. Adrian Croft, "Defense Cuts Jeopardize NATO's Effectiveness, Panetta Warns," *Reuters*, February 22, 2013.

42. George Will, "Some Questions for Hagel?" *Washington Post*, January 17, 2013.

43. John R. Deni, *The Future of American Landpower: Does Forward Presence Still Matter?: The Case of the Army in Europe*, Carlisle, PA: Strategic Studies Institute, U.S. Army War College, 2012, p. 2.

44. International Institute for Strategic Studies, *The Military Balance: 2013*, pp. 93-94.

45. Matthias Gebauer *et al.*, "European Obstruction: NATO Reforms Moving at 'Snail's Pace'," *Speigel Online*, February 25, 2013.

46. Gebauer, *et al.*

47. Lance M. Bacon, "Exiting Europe," *Army Times*, February 4, 2013.

48. For full details on cuts, base re-alignments, and timelines, see U.S. Department of Defense News Release, "DOD Announces U.S. Army in Europe Force Structure Changes," Washington, DC: DoD, March 1, 2013.

49. Bacon, "Exiting Europe."

50. "Thousands of Soldiers to Leave Europe," *Army Times*, March 1, 2013.

51. John Vandiver, "Pentagon Lays Out Significant Cut to U.S. Forces in Europe," *Stars and Stripes*, February 16, 2012.

52. *Ibid.* Overall, the U.S. European Command has cut more than 200 billets in management headquarters and an additional 150 from its intelligence directorate, and by 2012 had implemented a 15 percent decrease in personnel and budgets.

53. "Corker Agrees with Admiral Stavridis on Need for NATO Allies to Meet Commitments on Defense Spending," *The Chattanoogan*, March 16, 2013.

54. Lance M. Bacon, "Lawmakers Opt Against European Pullout, for Now," *Army Times*, February 3, 2013.

55. *Ibid.*

56. Gopal Ratnam, "NATO Readiness May be Hurt by U.S. Cuts, Official Says," *Bloomberg*, February 20, 2013.

57. For an early case on realigning the SACEUR position in Europe, see Charles Barry, Sean Kay, and Joshua Spero, "Completing the Transatlantic Bargain: The United States and European Security," *Current History*, Vol. 100, No. 644, March 2001, pp. 129-136.

58. See Sean Kay, *Celtic Revival? The Rise, Fall, and Renewal of Global Ireland*, Lanham, MD: Rowman and Littlefield, 2011. Also see Ben Tonra *et al.*, *Irish Foreign Policy*, London, UK: Gill and Macmillan, 2012.

59. General David M. Rodriguez, Statement before the Senate Armed Services Committee, Washington, DC, February 2013.

60. Thom Shanker, "U.S. and Allies Conduct Drills in Persian Gulf, Signal to Iran," *New York Times*, February 7, 2013.

61. Joshua Stewart and Sam Fellman, "Pentagon: U.S. Navy Carrier Fleet Cut to One in Gulf," *Defense News*, February 6, 2012.

62. Kori Schake, "The U.S. in Mali: Sniping from Behind?" *Foreign Policy.com*, January 23, 2013.

63. Adrian Croft, "Mali Shows Europe Must Work to Plug Defense Gaps: NATO," *Reuters*, January 31, 2013.

64. "Transcript: General Ham, Admiral Stavridis Testify Before House Armed Services Committee," Washington, DC, February 29, 2012.

65. The author is grateful for the off-the-record comments by a retired long-serving NATO expert currently consulting for the DoD.

66. See Joshua Spero, *Bridging the European Divide: Middle Power Politics and Regional Security Dilemmas*, Lanham, MD: Rowman and Littlefield, 2004.

67. "Sikorski: German Inaction Scarier than Germans in Action," *The Economist*, November 29, 2011.

68. Judy Dempsey, "Poland and France Move Toward a Europe Less Dependent on U.S.," *New York Times*, March 18, 2013.

69. For details on the seriousness of the Eurozone crisis for American stability, see Simon Johnson and Peter Boone, "The End of the Eurozone: A Survivor's Guide," available from *www.huffingtonpost.com/simon-johnson/euro-collapse_b_1549444.html*.

70. For details, see O'Donnell *et al*.

71. Naftali Bendavid and Adam Entous, "NATO Plea Gains Little Traction," *Wall Street Journal*, February 21, 2013.

72. Peter Grier, "NATO's Wobble," *Air Force Magazine*, February 2013, available from *www.airforce-magazine.com/ MagazineArchive/Pages/2013/February%202013/0213nato.aspx*.

73. Jeffrey Stacey, "The Era of Austerity or the Era of Intervention?" available from *www.whiteoliphaunt.com /duckofminerva/2013/02/the-era-of-austerity-or-the-era-of-intervention.html*.

74. Grier.

75. Ames, "Europe's Army."

76. John F. Burns, "British Military Expands Links to French Allies," *New York Times*, November 2, 2010.

77. *Ibid*.

78. The European Union has developed a "pooling and sharing" initiative which in 2011 identified 11 areas for joint capacity in important infrastructure categories like satellite communication. Additional areas include helicopter and pilot training, air-to-air refueling, and munitions. See International Institute for Strategic Studies, *The Military Balance: 2013*, p. 91.

79. *Ibid.*, p. 97. The draft White Paper indicated a growing need for a true European defense-industrial base for procurement based on competitive advantage and better coordination of research and development and European-level funding for defense investment.

80. Correspondence with Professor Lawrence S. Kaplan via email, March 2013.

81. Charlie Cooper, "Hammond: Europe Must Stop Relying on America," *The Independent*, November 2, 2012.

82. Michael Birnbaum, "Cuts in European Defense Budgets Raise Concerns for U.S., NATO," *Washington Post*, February 15, 2011.

83. "British Troops To Leave Germany by 2019," *Defense News*, March 5, 2013. The British will remove 11,000 troops back to the UK by 2016 and then all remaining 4,500 troops will depart Germany by 2019. This will cost the British government about 1 billion pounds to build housing for returning troops to be based in the UK and about 800 million pounds to be spent on infrastructure and base refurbishment.

84. "DoD Reviewing Strategy in Wake of Budget Cuts," *Defense News*, March 18, 2013.

ABOUT THE CONTRIBUTORS

CAROL ATKINSON is a Professor of the Practice of International Relations at the University of Southern California. In 2005, Dr. Atkinson completed a distinguished 26-year career in the U.S. Air Force. While in the military, she served in a wide range of operational assignments in the fields of intelligence, targeting, and combat assessment. During the fall of 2013 she was a Fulbright Senior Research Scholar at the G. S. Rakovski National Defense Academy in Sofia, Bulgaria. Dr. Atkinson's research focuses on how the United States extends its influence or "soft power" worldwide through military educational exchange programs hosted by U.S. elite military schools, its war and staff colleges. She recently completed a book on this topic called *Military Soft Power: Public Diplomacy Through Military Educational Exchanges* that will be available from Rowman & Littlefield in the spring of 2014. Dr. Atkinson teaches courses on U.S. national security, international politics, soft power, warfare and emerging threats, and the role of ideas, norms, and identity in international security. She is a graduate of the United States Air Force Academy, and holds a Ph.D. in political science from Duke University.

JOHN R. DENI joined the Strategic Studies Institute in November 2011 as a Research Professor of Joint, Interagency, Intergovernmental, and Multinational (JIIM) Security Studies. He previously worked for 8 years as a political advisor for senior U.S. military commanders in Europe. Prior to that, he spent 2 years as a strategic planner specializing in the military-to-military relationship between the United States and its European allies. While working for the U.S. military in Europe,

117

Dr. Deni was also an adjunct lecturer at Heidelberg University's Institute for Political Science. There, he taught graduate and undergraduate courses on U.S. foreign and security policy, North Atlantic Treaty Organization (NATO), European security, and alliance theory and practice. Before working in Germany, he spent 7 years in Washington, DC, as a consultant specializing in national security issues for the U.S. Departments of Defense, Energy, and State and has spoken at conferences and symposia throughout Europe and North America. Dr. Deni is the author most recently of the book, *Alliance Management and Maintenance: Restructuring NATO for the 21st Century*, as well as several journal articles. He has published op-eds in major newspapers such as the *Los Angeles Times* and the *Baltimore Sun*. Dr. Deni completed his undergraduate degree in history and international relations at the College of William & Mary and holds an M.A. in U.S. foreign policy at American University in Washington, DC, and a Ph.D. in international affairs from George Washington University.

SEAN KAY is Robson Professor of Politics and Government and Chair, International Studies at Ohio Wesleyan University. He is an Associate of the Mershon Center for International Security Studies at the Ohio State University, and a fellow in foreign policy and national security at the Eisenhower Institute in Washington, DC. He previously taught at Dartmouth College as visiting professor and was a research fellow at the Institute for National Strategic Studies at the National Defense University in Washington, DC. He is a frequent speaker and media commentator on American foreign and national security policy, with a focus on Europe and NATO. Dr. Kay is the author or co-editor of six books, including *NATO and the Future of European Security* and *Global Security in the Twenty-first Century: The Quest for Power and the Search for Peace*. His current book project focuses on contemporary strategic choices for American foreign and defense policy. Dr. Kay holds a B.A. and an M.A. from Kent State University, an M.A. from the Free University of Brussels, and a Ph.D. from the University of Massachusetts.

WILLIAM T. TOW is Professor and Head of the Department of International Relations in the School of International, Political and Strategic Studies (IPS), College of Asia & Pacific at the Australian National University (ANU). He directs the ANU's security component of the Australian Research Council's Centre for Excellence in Policing and Security. He has also co-managed the ANU's project on cross-comparing bilateral and multilateral security approaches in the Asia-Pacific as part of the MacArthur Foundation's Asian Security Initiative (MASI). He has served on the Foreign Affairs Council of Australia's Department of Foreign Affairs and Trade (DFAT), and the Board of Directors for the Australian-American Fulbright Commission. Dr. Tow has authored or edited 20 volumes or monographs and over 100 journal articles or book chapters on various aspects of Asian security relations and alliance politics. His books have become standard sources for analysts and students working on security issues in the Asia-Pacific. He was Editor for the *Australian Journal of International Affairs*. He is series co-editor for the Routledge Security in the Asia Pacific Series.

www.ingramcontent.com/pod-product-compliance
Lightning Source LLC
Chambersburg PA
CBHW071156280526
45787CB00002B/521